CORRECTIONS

No. 97   This painting was withdrawn from the exhibition by the lender.

No. 137   George Bellows did not exhibit with "The Eight" but became the most brilliant younger member of the Robert Henri "group" which formed the most important element in the "Eight."

No. 152a   *for:* Rio de Janeiro *read:* Morro

No. 250   *for:* Emile *read:* Emil

No. 274   *for:* George *read:* Georg

No. 323   *for:* Lent by the artist *read:* Lent by Miss Ruth Page, Chicago.

Page 289   Architecture and Industrial Art. *Add:* "The Evolution of the Skyscraper," a film prepared by the Department and photographed by E. Francis Thompson, will be shown in the auditorium throughout the period of exhibition.

The new building of the Museum of Modern Art, 11 W. 53rd Street, New York
Philip L. Goodwin, architect, Edward D. Stone, associated

ART IN OUR TIME

an
EXHIBITION
to celebrate the
TENTH ANNIVERSARY
of the
MUSEUM OF MODERN ART
and the opening of its
NEW BUILDING

held at the time of the
NEW YORK WORLD'S FAIR

1939

MUSEUM OF MODERN ART

CONTENTS

6

Out-of-Town Chairmen of the Membership Committee

Mrs. Thomas Robins, Jr., *Buffalo*, Mrs. Charles B. Goodspeed, *Chrm.*, *Chicago*, Mrs. Edward Byron Smith, *Vice-Chrm.*, *Chicago*, Mrs. William B. Hale, *Vice-Chrm.*, *Chicago*, Mrs. Ralph Burgess, *Colorado*, Mrs. Ernest Kanzler, *Detroit*, Mrs. Francis Goodwin, *Hartford*, Mrs. George A. Hill, Jr., *Houston*, Mrs. Robert Burgess, *Louisville*, Mrs. F. P. Heffelfinger, *Minneapolis*, Mrs. Campbell Howard, *Montreal*, Mrs. Gordon Sweet, *New Haven*, Mrs. Roger Thayer Stone, *New Orleans*, Mrs. Charles H. Chadwick, *Palm Beach*, Mr. Henry Clifford, *Philadelphia*, Mrs. George Liggett Craig, Jr., *Pittsburgh*, Mrs. William K. Prentice, *Princeton*, Mrs. Charles A. Robinson, Jr., *Providence*, Mrs. Francis Cunningham, *Rochester*, Mrs. William Mitchell, *St. Paul*, Mr. Joseph Winterbotham, *Vermont*, Mrs. Dwight Davis, *Washington*, Mrs. Elton S. Wayland, *Waterbury*

STAFF

Alfred H. Barr, Jr., *Director*

Thomas Dabney Mabry, Jr., *Executive Director*

Julian Street, Jr., *Secretary*

John McAndrew, *Curator of Architecture and Industrial Art*

Dorothy C. Miller, *Assistant Curator of Painting and Sculpture*

Beaumont Newhall, *Librarian*

Frances Collins, *Manager of Publications*

Elodie Courter, *Secretary of Circulating Exhibitions*

Sarah Newmeyer, *Director of Publicity*

Ione Ulrich, *Assistant to Executive Director*

Dorothy Dudley, *Registrar*

Monroe Wheeler, *Membership Director*

Janet Henrich, *Assistant, Architecture and Industrial Art*

Victor D'Amico, *Director of Educational Project*

John Ekstrom, *Superintendent of Building*

Ernest Tremp, *Assistant at Information Desk*

MUSEUM OF MODERN ART FILM LIBRARY

John E. Abbott, *Director*

Iris Barry, *Curator*

Florence West, *Executive Secretary*

Edward F. Kearns, *Technical Director*

Allen Porter, *Circulation and Exhibition Director*

Douglas Baxter, *Assistant to the Director*

Jay Leyda, *Assistant to the Curator*

William Jamison, *Field Investigator*

Helen Grey, *Stills*

Theodore Huff, *Music*

LENDERS TO THE EXHIBITION

Painting, Sculpture and Graphic Art

Saul Baizerman, New York
Josse and Gaston Bernheim-Jeune, Paris
Mrs. Cornelius N. Bliss, New York
Constantin Brancusi, Paris
Alexander Calder, New York
Mrs. Meric Callery, Boulogne-sur-Seine
Miss Mabel Choate, New York
Walter P. Chrysler, Jr., New York
Stephen C. Clark, New York
Ralph M. Coe, Cleveland
Erich Cohn, New York
The Cone Collection, Baltimore
Miss Louise Crane, New York
Frank Crowninshield, New York
Stuart Davis, New York
Mme. Jacques Doucet, Paris
Federal Art Project of the Works Progress
    Administration
Lyonel Feininger, New York
Marshall Field, New York
Edsel Ford, Dearborn
J. W. Freshfield, London
Naum Gabo, London
René Gaffé, Brussels
Mr. and Mrs. Ira Gershwin, Beverly Hills,
    California
Mrs. Rose Gershwin, New York
Philip Goodwin, New York
A. Conger Goodyear, New York
Mme. Cécile Gregory, Paris
Miss Adelaide M. De Groot, New York
Chaim Gross, New York
Mme. Paul Guillaume, Paris
Mme. E. Hostettler, Berne
Oscar Jespers, Brussels
T. Catesby Jones, New York
Mrs. Edgar Kaufmann, Pittsburgh
Mrs. David Levy, New York
The Lewisohn Collection, New York

Mme. Pierre Loeb, Paris
Miss Mary B. Lothrop, Boston
Henry P. McIlhenny, Germantown, Pa.
Dr. Franz Meyer, Zurich
Mrs. David M. Milton, New York
Henry Moore, London
Mrs. Randal Morgan, Chestnut Hill, Pa.
George L. K. Morris, New York
Mrs. James B. Murphy, New York
Christian Mustad, Oslo
Isamu Noguchi, New York
Frank and Robert Oppenheimer, Berke-
    ley, California
Frank Calvin Osborn, Manchester, Vt.
Walter Pach, New York
William S. Paley, New York
Mrs. John Parkinson, Jr., Westbury, N. Y.
Charles Prendergast, Westport, Conn.
Joseph Pulitzer, Jr., St. Louis
Mrs. Stanley Resor, New York
Edward G. Robinson, Beverly Hills, Cal.
Hugo Robus, New York
Mrs. John D. Rockefeller, Jr., New York
Nelson Rockefeller, New York
Mme. E. Ruckstuhl-Siegwart, Küssnacht-
    am-Rigi, Switzerland
Miss Antoinette Schulte, New York
John L. Sexton, Wilmington
Mr. and Mrs. Lesley Green Sheafer, New
    York
Mrs. John S. Sheppard, New York
James Thrall Soby, Farmington, Conn.
Maurice J. Speiser, Philadelphia
Mme. Sternheim, Paris
Miss Florine Stettheimer, New York
Alfred Stieglitz, New York
Miss Candace Stimson, New York
Mrs. Cornelius J. Sullivan, New York
Mrs. T. Durland Van Orden, New York

Mr. and Mrs. John W. Vandercook, New York

Edward M. M. Warburg, New York

Heinz Warneke, New York

Edwin S. Webster, Boston

Maurice Wertheim, New York

Mrs. Lloyd Bruce Wescott, Clinton, N. J.

Warren Wheelock, New York

John Hay Whitney, New York

Mrs. Payne Whitney, New York

Miss Gertrude B. Whittemore, Naugatuck, Connecticut

Dr. and Mrs. William Carlos Williams, Rutherford, New Jersey

William Zorach, New York

A. C. A. Gallery, New York

An American Place, New York

The Brummer Gallery, New York

Mme. Jeanne Bucher, Paris

Galerie Jeanne Bucher-Myrbor, Paris

Buchholz Gallery, New York

Carroll Carstairs, New York

The Downtown Gallery, New York

Marie Harriman Gallery, New York

C. W. Kraushaar Art Galleries, New York

Julien Levy Gallery, New York

Pierre Matisse Gallery, New York

J. B. Neumann, New York

Alfred Poyet, Paris

Frank K. M. Rehn Gallery, New York

Renou et Colle, Paris

Paul Rosenberg, Paris

Jacques Seligmann & Company, New York

Mrs. Cornelius J. Sullivan Gallery, New York

The Thannhauser Gallery, Paris

Walker Galleries, New York

The Weyhe Gallery, New York

Addison Gallery of American Art, Phillips Academy, Andover

Royal Museum of Fine Arts, Antwerp

The Museum of Fine Arts, Boston

Royal Museum of Fine Arts, Brussels

The Buffalo Fine Arts Academy, Albright Art Gallery, Buffalo

William Hayes Fogg Art Museum, Harvard University, Cambridge

The Art Institute of Chicago

The Cleveland Museum of Art

The Columbus Gallery of Fine Arts, Columbus, Ohio

The Detroit Institute of Arts

The Wadsworth Atheneum, Hartford

The Tate Gallery, London

The Gallery of Fine Arts, Yale University, New Haven

The Jeu de Paume Museum, Paris

Trustee of the John G. Johnson Collection, Philadelphia

The Philadelphia Museum of Art

The Toledo Museum of Art, Toledo, Ohio

The Corcoran Gallery of Art, Washington

Phillips Memorial Gallery, Washington

Photography

Berenice Abbott, New York

Ansel Adams, Yosemite National Park

Dr. Harold E. Edgerton, Cambridge, Mass.

Walker Evans, New York

David H. McAlpin, Princeton, New Jersey

James Thrall Soby, Farmington, Conn.

Ralph Steiner, New York

Films and Related Material

Walt Disney, Los Angeles

Mme. Germaine Dulac, Paris

Thomas A. Edison, Inc., East Orange, N. J.

Douglas Fairbanks, Sr., Santa Monica

J. S. Fairfax-Jones, London

Gaumont-Franco-Film-Aubert, Paris

D. W. Griffith, Los Angeles

William S. Hart, Newhall, California

Dmitri Kirsanov, Paris

Fernand Léger, Paris

The Jean A. LeRoy Collection

Harold Lloyd, Beverly Hills, Cal.

Loew's Inc., New York
Louis Lumière, Paris
Mrs. Philip Manson, New York
The March of Time, New York
Mme. Georges Méliès, Paris
Miss Mary Pickford, Hollywood
Paramount Pictures, Inc., New York
The Reichsfilmarchiv, Berlin
Mrs. Stella Simon, New York

Léopold Survage, Paris
Svensk Filmindustri, Stockholm
Twentieth Century-Fox Film Corp., New York
United Artists Corp., New York
Universal Pictures, Inc., New York
Universum-Film Aktiengesellschaft, Berlin
Warner Brothers Pictures, Inc., New York

In addition to those who have lent to the exhibition, the President and Trustees wish to thank the following for their assistance:

His Excellency Count Robert van der Straten-Ponthoz, Ambassador from Belgium; His Excellency William C. Bullitt, Ambassador of the United States to France; The Honorable Mrs. Florence J. Harriman, Minister of the United States to Norway; Mr. C. Oumansky, Chargé d'Affaires, Embassy of the Union of Soviet Socialist Republics, Washington; Mr. Alexander C. Kirk, Chargé d'Affaires, American Embassy, Moscow; The Honorable Robert Woods Bliss.

A. H. Cornette, Conservateur en chef, and Jozef Muls, Conservateur, of the Museum of Fine Arts, Antwerp; Leo van Puyvelde, Conservateur en Chef, and Arthur Haes, Conservateur, of the Museum of Fine Arts, Brussels; John Rothenstein, Director of the Tate Gallery, London; André Dezarrois, Conservateur, and Mlle. Rose Valland, of the Musée du Jeu de Paume, Paris.

Charles H. Sawyer, Curator of the Addison Gallery of American Art; Gordon Washburn, Director of the Albright Art Gallery; Henry E. Treide, President, and Charles R. Rogers, Assistant Director, of the Baltimore Museum of Art; George Harold Edgell, Director, and W. G. Constable, Curator of Paintings, of the Boston Museum of Fine Arts; Daniel Catton Rich, Director of Fine Arts of the Art Institute of Chicago; William M. Milliken, Director, and Henry Sayles Francis, Curator of Paintings, of the Cleveland Museum of Art; Philip Ryse Adams, Director of the Columbus Gallery of Fine Arts; C. Powell Minnigerode, Director of the Corcoran Gallery of Art; W. R. Valentiner, Director, and Clyde H. Burroughs, Secretary, of the Detroit Institute of Arts; Edward W. Forbes, Director of the Fogg Art Museum, Harvard University; Fiske Kimball, Director, and Henri Marceau, Assistant Director, of the Philadelphia Museum of Art; Duncan Phillips, Director of the Phillips Memorial Gallery; Blake-More Godwin, Director of the Toledo Museum of Art; A. Everett Austin, Jr., Director of the Wadsworth Atheneum; Theodore Sizer, Associate Director of the Gallery of Fine Arts, Yale University.

M. Jean Bernheim-Jeune; Mr. Henry Botkin; Mr. Francis Brennan; Mr. Joseph Brummer; Mr. Orville H. Bullitt; Mr. Arthur F. Egner; Mr. Lloyd Goodrich; Mr. T. J. Honeyman; Mr. Robert W. Macbeth; Mr. David H. McAlpin; Mr. Robert G. McIntyre; Dr. Franz Meyer; Mr. J. B. Neumann; Mr. Frank K. M. Rehn; M. Paul Rosenberg; Mr. S. Lewis Tim; Mr. Curt Valentin; Mr. Harris Whittemore, Jr.; Messrs. Wildenstein and Company; Mr. Carl Zigrosser.

PREFACE

In the tenth year of its existence the Museum of Modern Art comes of age, a precocious accomplishment. Reaching maturity it finds itself for the first time in a home of its own, designed for its special purposes with all of the advantages that the ingenuity of today and the experience of yesterday can devise.

The exhibition galleries provide three times the space available heretofore. In the offices the Museum staff for the first time has space to carry on its work properly and all of the Muesum's activities are now housed under one roof. The library emerges from its state of crowded confusion and is at last equipped for public use. An auditorium makes possible lectures, moving pictures and other developments. A final touch of completion is to be found in the garden which provides an outdoor display space as well as a setting for the building.

To mark this happy occasion the new building is opened with an exhibition illustrating our current activities. But this illustration is necessarily incomplete. The growth of the institution and its accomplishments during the past years can best be recited here.

The first intentions and purposes of the founders of the Museum have suffered surprisingly little change during the past ten years. We still remain primarily an educational institution. We adhere to the policy of holding temporary exhibitions illustrating the art of today and its derivations. We are acquiring a collection which will be permanent as a stream is permanent —with a changing content. The circulation of traveling exhibitions continues with increasing volume. As funds and personnel have permitted, new departments have been established—a Department of Architecture in 1932, to which was added Industrial Art in 1933, the Film Library in 1935. The foundations have been laid for enlarged activities in photography, the theatre arts, and public and private school education.

Since the opening of the Museum at 730 Fifth Avenue in the autumn of 1929 there have been one hundred and twelve temporary exhibitions with a total attendance of about 1,500,000 persons. Not all of those shows commanded a general acclaim; many were frowned upon by the ultra-conservatives; a few were scorned by advanced liberals. However, our aim has been to present to the public the living art of our own time and its sources and in this we may claim a reasonable success. Each year has seen at least one

11

exhibition that is memorable, from the showing of Cézanne, Gauguin, Seurat and van Gogh in 1929 to the presentation of *Three Centuries of Art in the United States* at the Museum of the Jeu de Paume in Paris last summer.

Our permanent collection was founded by the splendid bequest of Miss Lillie P. Bliss in 1931, and has been constantly added to by various gifts of which the principal one came from Mrs. John D. Rockefeller, Jr., in 1935.

In that same year the Film Library was founded and now has available for circulation over 1,000,000 feet of the great moving pictures of the past, most of which would otherwise be doomed to destruction.

Circulating exhibitions have increased in number from three shown fifteen times eight years ago to thirty-eight shown one hundred and forty-three times during the past season.

In its publications the Museum has conducted one of its most valuable services. Some fifty in number, they have been enthusiastically received by the general public and scholars alike.

With the facilities of the new building must come increasing service to the public, the more definite establishment of the Museum as a national institution devoted to increasing the esthetic content of our national life. To bring these things about, to enlarge upon our educational purposes, additional funds are required which should come principally from a greatly enlarged membership.

Private subscriptions made possible the program of the early years. With generous grants from the Carnegie and Rockefeller Foundations and a growing membership list these private subscriptions have continued. But the permanence and increasing service to which we look forward confidently will depend on the support that only a large membership can provide.

A. CONGER GOODYEAR, *President*

"ART IN OUR TIME"

THE PLAN OF THE EXHIBITION

"Art in Our Time" is the first exhibition in the Museum's new building; it celebrates the Tenth Anniversary of the Museum's foundation; and it is planned especially for the visitors to the New York World's Fair.

"Art in Our Time" presents achievements of living artists together with the work of certain important masters of yesterday. It differs from the special exhibitions of modern art in other New York museums at the time of the Fair by its inclusion of foreign work as well as American, and by its concern not only with painting, sculpture and the graphic arts but also with architecture, furniture, photography and moving pictures.

The Museum is keenly aware that visitors at the time of a World's Fair would be exhausted by any effort at academic completeness; and those who expect an elaborate and comprehensive survey may be disappointed for the exhibition offers really the minimum rather than the maximum of what the name implies. Such critics could logically suggest that the Museum change the title from "Art in Our Time" to "Some Aspects of the Visual Arts of Our Time and the Recent Past."

"Art in Our Time" (if we may still use the name) is planned along the general lines of the Museum's organization and is in fact intended to give some idea of the different kinds of art with which the Museum is concerned and some of the various ways of exhibiting them. The three main curatorial departments of the Museum—Painting and Sculpture, Architecture and Industrial Art, and the Film Library—are each represented by large divisions. Some departments which are not yet formally established, Graphic Arts, for instance, and Photography, are accorded smaller exhibitions, but other as yet unorganized departments such as Theatre Art and Commercial Art are not represented at all though the Museum has worked in these fields in the past and plans to be even more active in them in the near future.

Each department has chosen and presented its material in a different way. **Painting and Sculpture,** which occupies most of the Museum's gallery space, is divided about equally between American and European work of the past seventy years. This division is prefaced by a small but fine collection of **American Popular Art** of the past century and a half—painting and sculpture by the nonprofessional artist whose fresh, honest vision and unsophisticated technique has often produced work which is more exciting to the modern eye than that of any but the very best of his professional contemporaries. The room of American folk art will recall not only the much larger exhibition of similar material presented by the Museum in 1932, but also a series of exhibitions of the folk and primitive arts of other cultures—artistically important material which is still relegated for the most part to the museums of natural history.

After this prelude follow **American Painting of the Late 19th Century** and **European Painting of the Late 19th Century.** These seemed sufficiently different in character to be shown in separate chapters but the general homogeneity of international contemporary art suggested the inclusion in a single division of **20th Century Painting.** The art of watercolor painting, a medium in which at the present time our artists are very possibly preëminent, is represented by the work of **Six American Watercolorists,** without any European counterpart. The exhibition of paintings which begins with folk art is concluded with a group of **Paintings by Children** between the ages of eight and twelve, whose best work needs no apology and is, of course, directly related to the problem of recovering that innocence of eye and imaginative freedom desired by so many artists of our period. The painting and sculpture exhibition has in large part been selected in consultation with the Museum's Exhibition Committee.

Graphic art, the varied field of prints and drawings, is represented only in a most succinct form by a group of **Twenty-one Prints**—prints, however, which are for the most part as important in authorship as they are large in size. The exhibition of photography has also been focused upon a comparatively narrow and highly concentrated front comprising the work of **Seven American Photographers** who have come to the fore since the War.

The Museum is extremely fortunate in having its garden increased for the period of this exhibition to an area some 400 feet long by 100 deep. Divided between this "outdoor gallery" and an indoor gallery on the third floor are about sixty pieces representing **20th Century Sculpture and Constructions,** which range from figure sculpture in the classic tradition to surrealist dream palaces and windblown mobiles.

Good modern design in **Houses and Housing** is the subject chosen by the Department of Architecture and Industrial Art for its exhibition, which has been prepared in collaboration with the United States Housing Authority. For most visitors the design of the home, whether private house, apartment house, or large scale housing development, is the most personal and vital of all architectural problems. Especially at this moment is the question of good design in the last-named field urgently important because of the immense sum of $800,000,000 recently set aside by the government for the construction of low-rental housing projects throughout the country. This money is to be spent by municipalities, many of which through lack of training and experience are poorly equipped to cope with a problem which is as difficult architecturally as it is economically. The Museum is privileged to help in arousing public interest and cultivating public taste in what may be described as a national architectural emergency.

Exhibited in connection with the **Houses and Housing** show is a small group of modern chairs and a brilliant American design for a prefabricated "one-piece" bathroom. These few exhibits are in quantity little more than a symbol of the Museum's past work in industrial design which, as soon as plans mature, will be greatly augmented. The Department of Architecture and Industrial Art will also show its recently completed film on the evolution of the skyscraper.

The major part of the Film Library's exhibition is, of course, the **Cycle of Seventy Films.** These moving pictures, including a number of masterpieces chosen from a period of nearly half a century, will be shown in the auditorium in a series of some thirty programs. There will also be two special exhibitions of film material in the Museum's galleries, one devoted, as a demonstration of early 20th century archeology, to a pioneer producer of popular films; the other, by way of contrast, to what was probably the first project for an *avant-garde* film to be made entirely of animated abstract designs.

After the close of the exhibition the various departments, those already in existence and those in formation, will gradually be established in more or less permanent exhibition galleries on the second and third floors of the new building. Just how these galleries will be arranged will depend to a considerable degree upon the public's response to the present exhibition. Nothing that the visitors will see in the exhibition galleries, neither the works of art, nor the lighting fixtures, nor even the partitions, is at present permanent.

The Museum of Modern Art is a laboratory: in its experiments the public is invited to participate.

ALFRED H. BARR, JR., *Director*

15

1 KANE: Self Portrait. 1929. Oil on panel, 36 x 27 inches. The Museum of Modern Art, Mrs. John D. Rockefeller, Jr. Purchase Fund. *Illustrated also in color portfolio II* (*see* p. 379)

John Kane. American, born Scotland, 1859, of Irish parents. To America, 1880; lived in Pittsburgh. Self-taught; a house painter. Died Pittsburgh, 1934. See also no. 205.

AMERICAN POPULAR ART

American folk and popular art has received recognition only in recent years. Modern artists have been its "discoverers," finding in its clear childlike vision and straightforward technique qualities which they value. But though its discovery is the work of our generation, popular art has always been part of the background of American culture, as it has of European. Today machine civilization tends to destroy this background of folk tradition. But in art the vision of the common man continues to find expression in certain talented but untrained and isolated individuals—men who have found in themselves a kind of common pictorial language which links the American carpenter Pickett (no. 2) with the French gardener Bauchant (no. 203); Hicks, a Pennsylvania sign painter who died ninety years ago (nos. 5, 6) with the living color lithographer Peyronnet of Paris (no. 204); Bombois (no. 202) with the unknown master of the *Quilting Party* (no. 3); Kane's masterpiece (no. 1) with Rousseau's (no. 84).

This collection of American popular art is lent by Mrs. John D. Rockefeller, Jr.

D. C. M.

2   PICKETT: Manchester Valley. Probably 1914-1918. 45 x 60 inches. *Reproduced in color* (*see* p. 379)

Joseph Pickett. Born at New Hope, Pennsylvania, 1848. Carpenter and boat builder. Died at New Hope, 1918.

3 The Quilting Party. 1840-1850. Oil on wood, 13¼ x 25¼ inches
Found in Massachusetts.

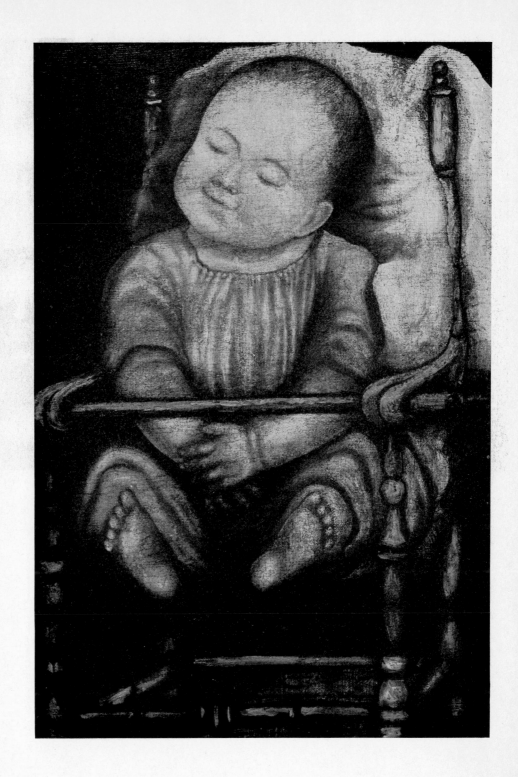

4 **Baby in Red High Chair.** About 1790. 21½ x 14¾ inches

Found in New York.

5   HICKS: The Residence of David Twining in 1787. 26½ x 31½ inches

Edward Hicks. Born at Attleborough, Pennsylvania, 1780. Quaker preacher who made his living as a coach maker and painter, and as a house and sign painter. Died at Newtown, Pennsylvania, 1849.

6 HICKS: The Peaceable Kingdom. About 1833. 17¼ x 23½ inches

7 Glass Bowl with Fruit. About 1820. Watercolor with tinsel, 17 x 13¾ inches
Found in Connecticut.

8　**Mourning Picture for Polly Botsford and Her Children.** About 1813. Watercolor, 19 x 24 inches

   The town of Botsford, Connecticut, was named after this family.

9　**Children and Governess.** 1800-1810. Watercolor, 14¾ x 17¾ inches. *Not illustrated*

   Found in Massachusetts.

10　**Horse.** Quill drawing with wash, 23¼ x 17 inches. *Not illustrated*

   An example of Pennsylvania German *fractur*, found in Bucks County.

11　Eagle. Wood, 68 inches high

Said to have been the sign for the Eagle Tavern, Pawtucket, Rhode Island.

12   Horse weathervane. Cast iron, 18 inches high

Found in Boston.

13   Rooster. Wood, 10½ inches high. *Not illustrated*

Pennsylvania German.

14   Rooster weathervane. Cast and cut-out iron, 23½ inches high. *Not illustrated*

Found in Boston.

15   Sheep weathervane. Stamped and cast copper, 31 inches long. *Not illustrated*

Found in Bucks County, Pennsylvania.

16   Cow weathervane. Stamped and cast copper, 28 inches long. *Not illustrated*

Found in Boston.

17-19   Toys: deer, dog, whale. Wood, 2¼ to 5 inches high. *Not illustrated*

Found in Chambersburg, Pennsylvania.

20   Seated Woman. Wood, 12 inches high. *Not illustrated*

Found near Ephrata, Pennsylvania.

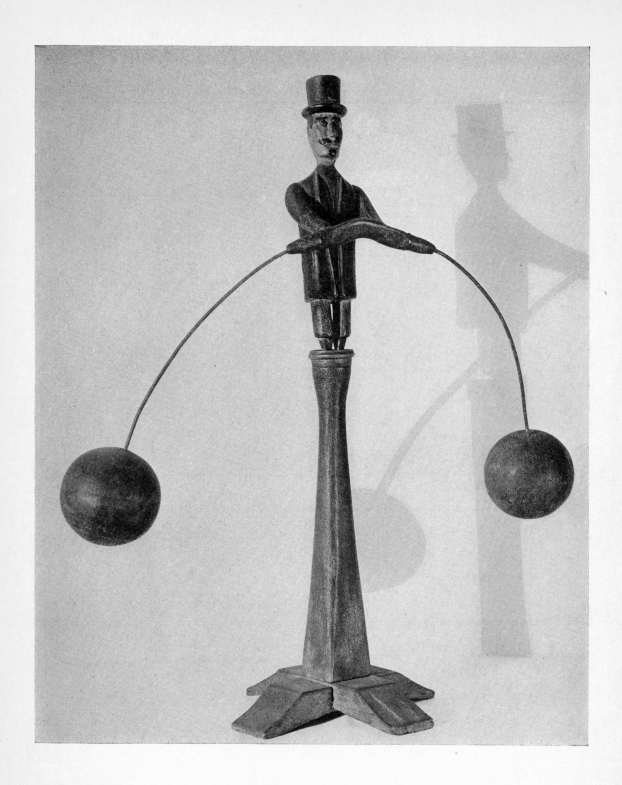

21 Balancing toy. Wood and metal, 15 inches high

Found in Pennsylvania.

22 Henry Ward Beecher. 1850-1860. Wood, 21 inches high

Said to have been carved by a farmer named Corbin at Centerville, Indiana, during a visit which Beecher made to Corbin's home.

24 Fish weathervane. Stamped and cut-out copper, 35½ inches long

Said to have been used on a church. Found in Massachusetts.

23 Bird. Wood, 12 inches long

Possibly a decoy. Found in New England.

AMERICAN PAINTING OF THE LATE 19TH CENTURY

The important trio formed by Ryder, the romantic, and the two realists, Homer and Eakins, come first; then, after La Farge and Harnett, follow the three expatriates, Whistler, Sargent and Mary Cassatt.

25   RYDER: Dead Bird. 1890-1900. Oil on wood, 4¼ x 9⅞ inches. Lent by the Phillips Memorial Gallery, Washington

26 RYDER: Death on a Pale Horse (The Race Track). 27¾ x 35¼ inches. Lent by the Cleveland Museum of Art

Albert Pinkham Ryder. American, 1847-1917. Ryder's scenes of romantic legend or clouded moonlight might have been banal had it not been for his mastery of design and his profound poetic feeling.

27   RYDER: The Temple of the Mind. 17¾ x 16 inches. Lent by the Buffalo Fine Arts Academy, Albright Art Gallery

28   RYDER: The Forest of Arden. 19 x 15 inches. Lent by Stephen C. Clark, New York

29 RYDER: Under a Cloud. 20 x 23¾ inches. Lent by Mrs. T. Durland Van Orden, New York

30 EAKINS: Starting out after Rail. 1874. 21½ x 20¼ inches. Lent by the Museum of Fine Arts, Boston

Thomas Eakins. American, 1844-1916. Lived in Philadelphia. He painted American people—sporting scenes, prize fights, rowing, hunting, hospital scenes and, above all, portraits which are remarkable for their ruthlessly honest penetration of character. Though grossly underestimated as an artist during his lifetime, his integrity has been an inspiration to many American painters during recent years.

31   EAKINS: John Biglen in a Single Scull. 1874. 24½ x 16¼ inches. Lent by the Gallery of Fine Arts, Yale University

32 EAKINS: Shad Fishing at Gloucester on the Delaware River. 1881. 12⅛ x 18¼ inches. Lent by the Philadelphia Museum of Art

33 EAKINS: Miss Van Buren. 1889. 45 x 41¾ inches. Lent by the Phillips Memorial Gallery, Washington

One of Eakins' most distinguished portraits.

33

34 **HOMER: Landscape with Figures.** About 1866. 24 x 38 inches. Lent by Stephen C. Clark

Winslow Homer. American, 1836-1910. Originally an illustrator for *Harper's Weekly*. Almost uninfluenced by his European contemporaries, he painted the American out-of-doors with simplicity, enthusiasm and unsurpassed power.

35 **HOMER: Dunes at Marshfield.** 1872. 13 x 21½ inches. Lent by Walker Galleries, New York

In recent years Homer's early pictures, most of them small in size, have been greatly admired for their color, quality of paint, and charm of subject, even though they lack the rather obvious power of the late sea pictures.

37 HOMER: Eight Bells. 1888. 24¼ x 30½ inches. Lent by the Addison Gallery of American Art, Phillips Academy, Andover

36 HOMER: The Croquet Match. 1872. Oil on academy board, 9¾ x 15½ inches. Lent by Edwin S. Webster, Boston. *Illustrated in color portfolio I (see p. 378)*

38 HOMER: Summer Night. 1890. 29½ x 39¾ inches. Lent by the Jeu de Paume Museum, Paris

39 HOMER: Coast in Winter. 1890. 35¼ x 30¾ inches. Lent by the Trustee of the John G. Johnson Collection, Philadelphia

40 HOMER: Kissing the Moon. 1904. 30¼ x 40¼ inches. Lent by Miss Candace Stimson, New York

41 **HOMER: Right and Left.** 1909. 28⅜ x 48½ inches. Lent by Mrs. Randal Morgan, Chestnut Hill

42   LA FARGE: Paradise Valley, Newport. About 1872. 34 x 43 inches. Lent by Miss Mary B. Lothrop, Boston

John La Farge. American, 1835-1910. Known for his mural and stained glass compositions, such as the large panel in the Church of the Ascension, at Fifth Avenue and 10th Street, New York, which show his great knowledge of Italian Renaissance art. His occasional American landscapes are among his best paintings.

43 HARNETT: Old Scraps. 1879-1880? 30 x 25 inches. Lent by the Downtown Gallery, New York

William Michael Harnett. American, born Cork County, Ireland, 1848. To America, 1849. Lived chiefly in Philadelphia. Died New York City, 1892. His paintings such as the *Old Scraps* curiously anticipate certain experiments of the Cubists in combining various real and imitation textures in a flat angular composition. The uncanny illusionistic character of his technique reappears again in many Surrealist *trompe-l'oeil* (fool-the-eye) paintings, notably those of Pierre Roy, no. 191.

44 WHISTLER: The Coast of Brittany. 1861. 35 x 46 inches. Lent by the Wadsworth Atheneum, Hartford

James Abbott McNeill Whistler. American, 1834-1903. After early studies in Paris he lived in London where he fought English philistinism with vitriolic wit. His work seemed so revolutionary that in 1878, seven years after he had painted his now beloved portrait of his mother, John Ruskin, the leading English critic, called one of his *Nocturnes* a "paint pot flung in the face of the public." His early *Coast of Brittany* is under Courbet's influence.

45 WHISTLER: The White Girl. 1862. 84¾ x 42¼ inches. Lent by Miss Gertrude B. Whittemore, Naugatuck

Now one of the most admired Whistlers, this portrait was once considered so radical that it was refused exhibition at the English Royal Academy of 1862. It was rejected again at the official French *Salon* of 1863, but was given a place of honor in the famous Paris *Salon des Refusés* of the same year, along with the rejected works of other rebels such as Manet and Pissarro.

45

46 SARGENT: Mrs. Charles Gifford Dyer. 1880. 24½ x 17 inches. Lent by the Art Institute of Chicago

47   SARGENT: Robert Louis Stevenson. 1885. 20¼ x 24¼ inches. Lent by Mrs. Payne Whitney, New York

John Singer Sargent. American, 1856-1925. Lived mostly in France and England. For many years the world's most fashionable portrait painter. Some of his more modest early works, such as the portraits of Stevenson and of Mrs. Dyer, are among his best.

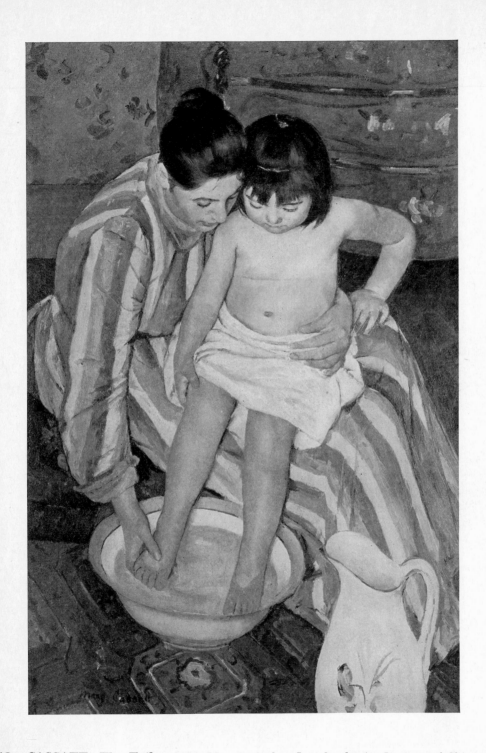

48 CASSATT: The Toilet. 1894. 39 x 26 inches. Lent by the Art Institute of Chicago

Mary Cassatt. American, 1845-1926. Lived in France. She exhibited with the French Impressionists and was admired by them, especially by Degas. Like them she was influenced by Japanese prints. Compare her etching, no. 241.

EUROPEAN PAINTING OF THE LATE 19TH CENTURY

The two great masters Renoir and Cézanne are followed by seven painters of a slightly younger generation whose art came to maturity in the 1880's and 90's: Gauguin, Seurat, Toulouse-Lautrec and Redon were French, van Gogh a Hollander, Ensor a Belgian, Munch a Norwegian, but artistically they were related in many ways. Comparatively independent were Rousseau, the French toll collector, and Greaves, the English boatman's son, simple men who painted pictures without much regard for movements and traditions.

49 **RENOIR: Le Moulin de la Galette.** 1876. 30½ x 44¼ inches. Lent by John Hay Hay Whitney, New York. *Illustrated in color portfolio I* *(see p. 378)*

Either this painting of a Paris outdoor café, or a larger version of the same subject now in the Louvre, was sent to the Impressionist exhibition of 1877, of which an exasperated critic wrote: "When children amuse themselves with paper and colors, they do better." Sixty years ago the general public thought the Impressionists were either crazy or incompetent, because instead of painting a conventional imitation of natural detail they tried to capture changing effects of light and atmosphere by using dabs of bright, shimmering color.

Auguste Renoir. French, 1841-1919. His youthful works of the 1870's are the finest Impressionist paintings. Later under the influence of old masters like Rubens and Titian, his art became richer in color and more rhythmic in form until it sings in a ripe, full-throated, luxuriant harmony.

50 RENOIR: Luncheon of the Boating Party. 1881. 51 x 68 inches. Lent by the Phillips Memorial Gallery, Washington

This is the greatest and one of the last of Renoir's Impressionist paintings.

51　RENOIR: Little Margot Bérard. 1879. 16 x 12⅝ inches. Lent by Stephen C. Clark, New York. *Reproduced, Museum of Modern Art Color Print No. 3* *(see p. 380)*

52 RENOIR: Three Bathers. 1897. 21⅜ x 25¾ inches. Lent by Ralph M. Coe, Cleveland
The swinging Baroque rhythms of Renoir's later work continue the grand tradition of Rubens and Delacroix.

53 RENOIR: The Judgment of Paris. 1910. 28¾ x 36¼ inches. Lent by Mme. Paul Guillaume, Paris

To express his profound joy in nature Renoir in his late work amplified the forms and intensified the colors of what he painted, whether landscape, fruit and flowers, or women's bodies.

54 RENOIR: Gabrielle at the Mirror. 1910. 32 x 25½ inches. Lent by Josse and Gaston Bernheim-Jeune, Paris

55 CEZANNE: The Black Clock. 1869-1871. 21¾ x 29¼ inches. Lent by Edward G. Robinson, Beverly Hills

In his early work Cézanne often spread the paint on with a knife, achieving almost by brute strength a rich and vigorous effect.

Paul Cézanne. French, 1838-1906. Influenced first by Daumier, Delacroix, Courbet and Renaissance and Baroque masters, and later by Manet, Pissarro and the Impressionists with whom he exhibited.

Cézanne in his own words tried to make of Impressionism something solid and lasting "like the art of the museums." He wanted to get back to the traditions of the old masters without sacrificing the new technique of vibrating color which the Impressionists of the 1870's had developed. In attempting to solve this problem he became one of the greatest and probably the most influential artist of the last 100 years.

56 CEZANNE: Man in a Blue Cap (Uncle Dominic). About 1865. 31⅜ x 25¼ inches. The Museum of Modern Art, the Lillie P. Bliss Collection. *Illustrated in color portfolio I; also in color on postcard (see pp. 378, 380)*

A crudely powerful early portrait painted under Courbet's influence.

57   CEZANNE: Cherries and Peaches. 1883-1887. 19¾ x 24 inches. Lent anonymously

Even without its other more important virtues, Cézanne's art would live because of its frequently superb color.
Compare with the *Black Clock*, opposite, of 15 years earlier.

58   CEZANNE: L'Estaque. 1886-1890. 31½ x 39 inches. Lent by William S. Paley, New York

The extraordinary sense of ordered space in Cézanne's landscapes can be felt only after some minutes of study. This is a work of Cézanne's middle period when he was especially interested in the study of deep space.

59   CEZANNE: Pines and Rocks. About 1895-1900. 31⅞ x 25⅞ inches. The Museum of Modern Art, the Lillie P. Bliss Collection

A late landscape in which Cézanne shuts out deep space and paints instead a curtain of angular forms which anticipated—and actually influenced—the more abstract compositions of the Cubists. See Picasso, no. 157; Léger, no. 169; La Fresnaye, no. 174.

60   CEZANNE: Mme. Cézanne in the Conservatory. 1891. 36½ x 28½ inches. Lent by Stephen C. Clark, New York

Compare the thin transparent paint and sensitive color of this mature work with the thickly plastered surface of the *Uncle Dominic*, no. 56, of 30 years before.

61   CEZANNE: Still Life with Apples. About 1891-1893. 26⅞ x 36½ inches. The Museum of Modern Art, the Lillie P. Bliss Collection

62 CEZANNE: The Card Players. 1892. 25⅝ x 32½ inches. Lent by Stephen C. Clark, New York. *Reproduced, Museum of Modern Art Color Print No. 2 (see p. 380)*

In his long series of *Card Players*, Cézanne concentrated his power of building a composition until it suggests the strength of architecture. Compare the lithograph of the *Bathers*, no. 240.

63 CEZANNE: Old Woman with a Rosary. 1900-1904. 33½ x 25½ inches. Lent by Mme.
Jacques Doucet, Paris

Cézanne was so much interested in the technique and esthetic problems of form that he usually overlooked the
state of mind and even the character of his sitters, requiring them merely to sit "as still as an apple." A remarkable exception to this attitude is the *Old Woman with a Rosary*, done toward the end of Cézanne's life and here
shown for the first time in America.

64 **GAUGUIN: Three Dogs, Three Wineglasses, Three Apples.** 1888. Oil on wood, 36 x 24½ inches. Lent by Mme. Sternheim, Paris, courtesy Paul Rosenberg

Gauguin is reported by one of his English acquaintances to have admired the flat, decorative, unpretentious children's illustrations of Kate Greenaway, whose work may have influenced this curiously innocent composition.

Paul Gauguin. French, 1848-1903. Gave up a successful business career for art and then abandoned civilization to paint in the South Seas, where he died. Under the influence of primitive and folk art he tried to make painting simple, direct, and decorative in reaction against the elaborate semi-scientific attitude of Impressionism.

65 GAUGUIN: Calvary. 1889. 36¼ x 29 inches. Lent by the Royal Museum of Fine Arts, Brussels

Gauguin greatly esteemed the crudely sincere religious sculpture of the peasants of Brittany. Later, he **was to** seek the stimulation of the even more primitive art and life of the South Seas.

66 GAUGUIN: The Spirit of the Dead Watching (Manaò Tupapaù). 1892. 28¾ x 36¼ inches. Lent by A. Conger Goodyear, New York. *Illustrated in color portfolio I (see p. 378)*

Gauguin has left his own notes about this masterpiece, which represents the Tahitian spirit of the dead watching a young girl. He concluded his analysis with these words: "The musical part: undulating horizontal lines, harmonies of orange and blue woven together by yellows and violets, their complementary colors, and lightened by greenish sparkles. The literary part: the Spirit of a Living Girl united with the Spirit of the Dead. Night and Day.

"This explanation of the genesis of my picture is written for the benefit of those who always insist on knowing the why and wherefore of everything.

"Otherwise it is simply no more than a study of the nude in Oceania."

67 GAUGUIN: We Greet You, Mary (Ia Orana Maria). 1891. 44¾ x 34½ inches. Lent by the Lewisohn Collection, New York

One of the most elaborate and decorative paintings of Gauguin's first visit to Tahiti; the subject is a poetic translation into Tahitian terms of the traditional *Adoration of the Shepherds.*

IA ORANA MARIA

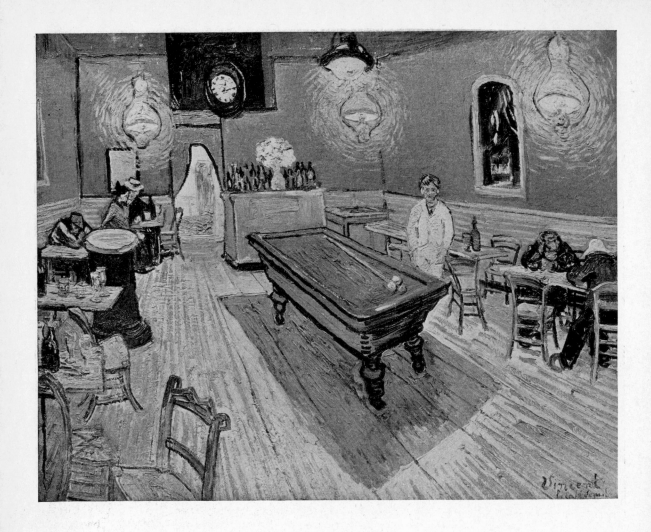

68 VAN GOGH: Night Café. Arles, 1888. 28¾ x 36⅛ inches. Lent by Stephen C. Clark, New York

In letters to his brother Theo, van Gogh described this masterpiece:

"In my picture of the *Night Café* I have tried to express the idea that the café is a place where one can ruin one's self, run mad or commit a crime. So I have tried to express as it were the powers of darkness in a low drink shop, by soft Louis XV green and malachite, contrasting with yellow green and hard blue greens, and all this in an atmosphere like a devil's furnace, of pale sulphur." (Letter 534)

"Exaggerated studies like the *Sower*, and like this *Night Café*, seem to me usually atrociously ugly and bad, but when I am moved by something, as now by this little article on Dostoievsky, then these are the only ones which appear to have any deep meaning." (Letter 535)

Vincent van Gogh. Dutch, 1853-1890. Worked in France, 1886-1890. Distraught by his inability to adjust his life or his art to an unsympathetic world, he killed himself. Today the world honors his martyrdom and loves his vibrant emotional pictures which 50 years ago seemed repulsive and incomprehensible.

69 VAN GOGH: L'Arlésienne (Mme. Ginoux). Arles, 1888. 36 x 29 inches. Lent by the Lewisohn Collection, New York. *Illustrated in color portfolio I* (*see p. 378*)

To his brother Theo, van Gogh wrote: "I have an Arlésienne at last, a figure slashed on in an hour, background pale lavender, the face grey, the clothes black, black, black, with perfectly raw Prussian blue. She is leaning on a green table and seated in an armchair of orange wood." (Letter 559)

This painting, now one of the most generally admired pictures in the United States, was so little understood when it was painted that van Gogh wrote to his brother: "I am pleased, too, to hear that someone else has turned up who actually saw something in the woman's figure, in black and yellow . . . though I think that the merit is in the model and not in my painting." (Letter 595)

70 VAN GOGH: Hills at Saint-Rémy. Saint-Rémy, 1889. 28¾ x 36¼ inches. Lent by the Thannhauser Gallery, Paris

71 VAN GOGH: Sunset over Ploughed Fields. Saint-Rémy, 1890. 28¾ x 36½ inches. Lent anonymously

72 VAN GOGH: Portrait of Mlle. Ravoux. Auvers, 1890. 25¾ x 21⅜ inches. Lent anonymously

To his brother Theo, van Gogh wrote: "Last week I did a portrait of a girl of 16 or nearly, in blue against a blue background, the daughter of the people where I am staying. I have given her this portrait, but I made a variation of it for you." (Letter 644)

73 **VAN GOGH: Fields at Auvers.** Auvers, 1890. 29⅝ x 37¼ inches. Lent by Marshall Field, New York

74 SEURAT: Sunday on the Grande-Jatte. 1885-1886. 27¾ x 41 inches. Lent by the Lewisohn Collection, New York

This is the final and nearly complete study for the painting in the Art Institute of Chicago which is one of the masterpieces of European painting. The *Sunday on the Grande-Jatte* is the second of Seurat's six major works. It was composed with the most painstaking care after innumerable studies of details. The deep perspective is staked out in a rhythmic recession of planes, almost as deliberately as if it were a chessboard on which the pieces are human beings.

Georges Seurat. French, 1859-1891. Worked in Paris after 1880. Seurat's brief career as an artist was dominated by a passion for system and order. With a scientific precision he took the small brush strokes of the Impressionists and made them into dots all of the same size. Each dot is a light or dark shade of one of the six pure, primary colors—blue, yellow, red, green, violet and orange. With similar logic he analyzed lines and tones and their emotional effects of sadness, calm, and joy. Though his method seems over-scientific, Seurat painted several of the greatest compositions of modern times. To artists of today he is the supreme example of intelligence and discipline. Of his six major works one, *The Side Show*, is included, together with the final studies for two others.

75 **SEURAT: The Models** (Les Poseuses). 1887-1888. 15½ x 19½ inches. Lent by Henry P. McIlhenny, Germantown

The final study for the large canvas in the collection of the Barnes Foundation, Merion, Pa.

76 SEURAT: The Side Show (La Parade). 1889. 39½ x 59½ inches. Lent by Stephen C. Clark, New York

The fourth of Seurat's six great pictures. In comparison with the *Grande-Jatte* deep space is abandoned for a flat vertical composition, almost like a Byzantine mosaic or an Egyptian wall painting. In this magnificent picture, Seurat's laboriously scientific technique dissolves the natural forms into a kind of molecular dance and achieves at the same time an unearthly radiation of light.

77 TOULOUSE-LAUTREC: The Black Countess. 1881. Oil on cardboard, 12¼ x 15 inches.
Lent by Maurice Wertheim, New York

Count Henri de Toulouse-Lautrec. French, 1864-1901. Crippled in early youth, he assumed the rôle of an observer and used his serpent-like line to record with penetration and acid irony the life of Paris: race courses, night clubs and circuses. *The Black Countess* is an early picture under Impressionist influence.

78 **TOULOUSE-LAUTREC: In the Fernando Circus: the Ring Master.** 1888. 38¾ x 63½ inches. Lent by the Art Institute of Chicago

79 TOULOUSE-LAUTREC: At the Moulin Rouge: the Dance. 1890. 45¼ x 59 inches. Lent by Henry P. McIlhenny, Germantown

80 REDON: The Chariot of Apollo. Oil on wood, 29½ x 18¾ inches. Lent by Mrs. Cornelius N. Bliss, New York

Odilon Redon. French, 1840-1916. He painted myths, flowers, butterflies, and dreams.

81   REDON: Vase of Flowers. 1916. Pastel, 34 x 21½ inches. Lent by William S. Paley, New York

82 ENSOR: Intrigue (Masks). 1890. 35½ x 59 inches. Lent by the Royal Museum of Fine Arts, Antwerp

Baron James Ensor. Belgian, born 1860. Lives in Ostend. A pioneer during the 1880's and 90's of modern fantastic art and the foremost living Belgian artist.

83 MUNCH: The Storm. 1893. 38½ x 50 inches. Lent by Christian Mustad, Oslo.

Edvard Munch. Norwegian, born 1863. Lives near Oslo. A contemporary of Seurat and Toulouse-Lautrec, Munch remains the most important artist of modern Scandinavia, having exerted a great influence upon the painting and graphic art of Northern Europe and especially upon German Expressionism. His work of the 1890's was remarkable both for its boldness of form and its romantic melancholy. See also his lithograph, no. 244.

84 **ROUSSEAU: The Sleeping Gypsy** (La Bohémienne Endormie). 1897. 79 x 51 inches. Lent by Mme. E. Ruckstuhl-Siegwart, Küssnacht-am-Rigi, Switzerland

The Sleeping Gypsy is generally considered one of Rousseau's masterpieces. In no other picture does he achieve to such a degree the vivid, trancelike immobility of a dream.

85 **ROUSSEAU: Joseph Brummer.** 1909. 45¾ x
35 inches. Lent by Dr. Franz Meyer, Zurich

This is a portrait of a well known American art dealer,
who, together with the American painter Max Weber (see
no. 124), knew Rousseau well in the last years of his life.

Henri Rousseau. French, 1844-1910. Called "le Douanier"
because of his job as a minor customs officer. Greatest of
the many "modern primitives," self-taught artists of the
people, whose fresh eye, untutored technique and imaginative power have interested modern artists. Compare
nos. 2, 3, 203, 205.

86 GREAVES: Hammersmith Bridge on Boat-race Day. 36 x 55 inches. Lent by the Tate Gallery, London

Walter Greaves. English, 1846-1931. A naïve bohemian eccentric who as a boy was befriended by Whistler. He insisted, however, that this, his master-piece, was painted before he came to know Whistler, that is, at about the age of 15. In any case Whistler's influence is very slight in a painting which resembles that of the self-taught "popular" artists.

20TH CENTURY PAINTING

Painters who seem to share a generally
similar character or interest are grouped
together, without any emphasis on historical order or national division. For instance, the painters who work in the Impressionist tradition (nos. 87-90) or seem
primarily interested in American local
color (nos. 137-149) or in fantastic inventions and juxtapositions (nos. 182-
201) are placed roughly in sequence
without implying a strict classification.

87 VUILLARD: Portrait of Lugné Poë.
1891. 8½ x 10 inches. Lent by Miss
Mabel Choate, New York

Jean Edouard Vuillard. French, born 1868.
Lives in Paris. Influenced by Degas and Toulouse-Lautrec. Developed a personal, intimate
kind of indoor Impressionism which places
him, with Rouault, Bonnard and Matisse, at
the top of the oldest generation of living
French painters.

88 VUILLARD: Mother and Sister of the Artist. About 1900. $18\frac{1}{4}$ x $22\frac{1}{4}$ inches. The Museum of Modern Art, gift of Mrs. Sadie A. May

89 BONNARD: The Breakfast Room. 62¼ x 43 inches. Lent by Stephen C. Clark, New York.
Illustrated in color portfolio I (see p. 378)

Pierre Bonnard. French, born 1867. Lives in Paris. With Vuillard, the greatest living French master of the Impressionist tradition, which he has enriched by his superb color and his feeling for intimate atmosphere.

90   PRENDERGAST: Acadia. About 1917. 32½ x 37½ inches. Lent by the C. W. Kraushaar Art Galleries, New York

Maurice Prendergast. Born at St. John's, Newfoundland, 1859. Died in New York, 1924. Exhibited in New York in 1908 with the revolutionary group, "The Eight." Influenced by Cézanne and Signac, he employed a highly personal and distinguished kind of decorative Impressionism.

91 **MATISSE: The Dance.** 1909-1910. 108 x 144 inches. Lent by Walter P. Chrysler, Jr., New York

Henri-Matisse. French, born 1869. Lives in Nice. Matisse in 1905 was the leader of the *Fauves* (wild beast) group who went beyond Gauguin in using bright flat color and heavy black outlines. *The Dance* is a full-sized study for the decoration completed for Shchukine, a Moscow banker, in 1910. Of this famous picture Matisse wrote that it was done "with a beautiful blue for the sky, the bluest of blues" to which was added "the green of the grass and the vibrant vermilion of the bodies."

92 MATISSE: Olga (Femme au Corsage Vert). 1910. 39½ x 32 inches. Lent by Walter P. Chrysler, Jr., New York

93 **MATISSE: The Blue Window.** About 1912. 51¼ x 35⅛ inches. Lent anonymously

94 **MATISSE: Goldfish.** 1915-1916. Lent by Mme. Jacques Doucet, Paris

One of the notable paintings of a period in which Matisse, slightly influenced by Cubism, produced some of his strongest and most austere works.

95 **MATISSE: White Plumes.** 1919. 29 x 24 inches. Lent by Stephen C. Clark, New York. *Illustrated in color portfolio I (see p. 378)*

96   MATISSE: Girl in a Yellow Dress. 1929-1931. 39⅜ x 32 inches. Lent by the Cone Collection, Baltimore

Thirty years ago Matisse wrote: "What I dream of is an art of balance, of purity and serenity devoid of troubling and depressing subject matter . . ."

97 DUFY: Nice. 1928. 23½ x 29 inches. Lent by Carroll Carstairs, New York

Raoul Dufy. French, born 1879. Lives in Paris. Gay in spirit, brilliant in technique.

98   DERAIN: Valley of the Lot at Vers. 1912. 28¾ x 36⅛ inches. Lent anonymously

André Derain. French, born 1880. Lives in Paris. Derain's early work was influenced by many sources, including Negro sculpture, Cézanne, as in no. 98, and medieval Italian frescoes, as in no. 99. After the War, through his adaptation of the French tradition of Courbet, as in no. 100, and Corot, he exerted a wide influence upon younger men.

99   DERAIN: Portrait of the Artist. 1912. 45¾ x 35 inches. Lent by the Pierre Matisse Gallery,
New York

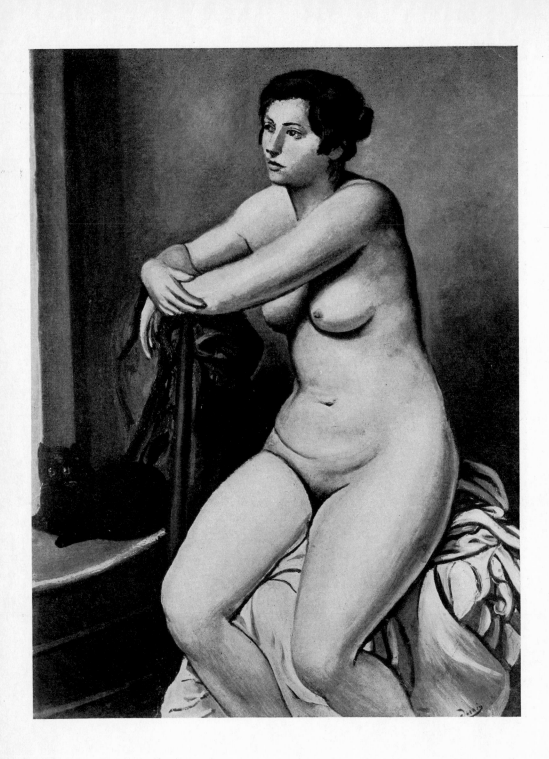

100   DERAIN: Nude with Cat. 1923. 45¾ x 35 inches. Lent by Renou et Colle, Paris

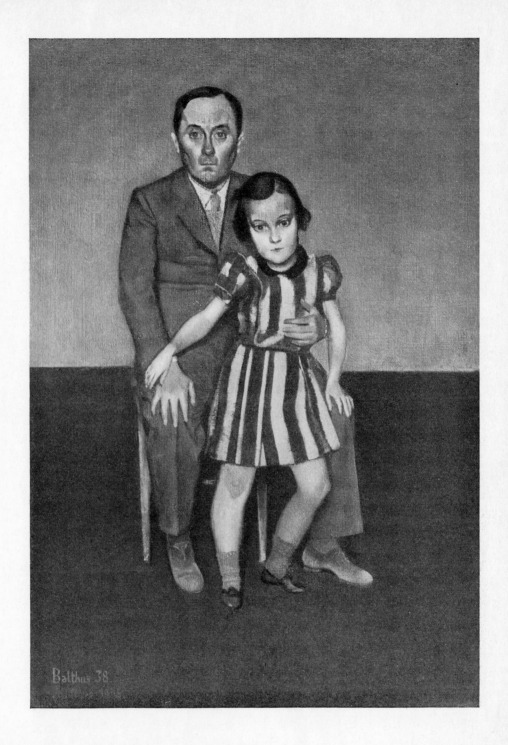

101 BALTHUS: Joan Miro and His Daughter Dolores. 1937-1938. 51¼ x 35 inches. The
Museum of Modern Art, Mrs. John D. Rockefeller, Jr. Purchase Fund

Balthus (Balthasar Klossowsky). French, born of Polish ancestry, 1910. Lives in Paris. Influenced by Courbet
and Derain. For Miro's painting see no. 196.

102 **MODIGLIANI: Reclining Nude.** 28¾ x 45¾ inches. Lent by Jacques Seligmann & Company, New York

Amedeo Modigliani, Italian, 1884-1920. Worked in Paris, where he died. Influenced by Negro sculpture and by Italian masters such as Botticelli, his work is distinguished especially for its pure, sweeping outline.

103 **MODIGLIANI: Blaise Cendrars.** 24 x 19¾ inches. Lent by Alfred Poyet Gallery, Paris

Cendrars was a poet and friend of the artist.

104 UTRILLO: Chartres Cathedral. 1913. 35¾ x 19½ inches. Lent by Mrs. Lloyd Bruce Wescott, Clinton, N. J.

Maurice Utrillo. French, born 1883. Lives in Paris. Utrillo probably painted his *Chartres* in his studio, possibly using a postcard or photograph for a model.

105 **SOUTINE: Chartres Cathedral.** 1933. Oil on wood, 36 x 19½ inches. Lent by Mrs. Lloyd Bruce Wescott, Clinton, N. J.

Chaim Soutine. Born Lithuania, 1884. Lives in Paris. Remarkable for the richness and vitality of his brushwork. His *Chartres*, unlike Utrillo's, was painted only after many hours of concentrated study of the cathedral itself.

106 KOKOSCHKA: The Elbe River near Dresden. 1920. 31¾ x 44 inches. Lent by the Buchholz
Gallery, New York

Oskar Kokoschka. Born 1886. Austrian Czech by birth and education but lived in Berlin and Dresden until 1933;
recently in Prague; now in London. The foremost Central European painter.

107   **MARIN: Off Cape Split, Maine.** 1938. 21¾ x 28 inches. Lent by An American Place, New York

John Marin. Born Rutherford, N. J., 1870. Associated with Alfred Stieglitz. Lives at Cliffside, N. J. His recent oil paintings are beginning to share the great esteem in which his watercolors are held. In their bold vehement brushwork and emotional intensity they bear an interesting relationship to the work of Soutine and Kokoschka.

108 DAVIES: Italian Landscape. 1925. 25½ x 39½ inches. The Museum of Modern Art, the Lillie
P. Bliss Collection

Arthur B. Davies. Born Utica, N. Y., 1862. Died Italy, 1928. Led in organizing "Armory Show," New York,
1913, and greatly encouraged the patronage of modern art in New York.

109 STERNE: The Winding Path. 1922. 45¾ x 34 inches. Lent by the Lewisohn Collection, New York

Maurice Sterne. American, born Latvia, 1877. To New York, 1889. Painted in Italy and Bali. Lives in California.

110 EILSHEMIUS: Plaza Theatre. 1915. Oil on composition board, 30½ x 40⅝ inches. Lent by Mr. and Mrs. Ira Gershwin, Beverly Hills

Louis Eilshemius. Born near Newark, N. J., 1864. Studied with Kenyon Cox, New York, 1882; Bouguereau, Paris, 1888. Lives in New York.

111   **KARFIOL: Making Music.** 1938. 34 x 40 inches. Lent by the Downtown Gallery, New York

Bernard Karfiol. Born near Budapest, 1886, of American parents. Lives in New York.

112 **KUNIYOSHI: Self Portrait as Golf Player.** 1927. 50 x 40¼ inches. The Museum of Modern Art, Mrs. John D. Rockefeller, Jr. Purchase Fund

Yasuo Kuniyoshi. Born Japan, 1893. Lives in New York.

113   BROOK: A Number of Things. 1935. 32 x 48 inches. Lent by the Museum of Fine Arts, Boston
Alexander Brook. Born Brooklyn, 1898. Lives in New York.

114   McFEE: Leaves and Apples. 1932. 24 x 30 inches. Lent by Mr. and Mrs. Lesley Green Sheafer, New York

Henry Lee McFee. Born St. Louis, 1886. Lives in Woodstock, N. Y.

115   JOHN: Eve Kirk. 1929. 36 x 23¾ inches. Lent by J. W. Freshfield, London. *Not illustrated (no photograph available)*

Augustus John. English, born 1878. The most brilliant of the older generation of English **painters.**

116 SPEICHER: Katharine Cornell as *Candida*. 1925-1926. 84 x 44½ inches. The Museum of Modern Art, gift of Miss Katharine Cornell

Eugene Speicher. Born Buffalo, N. Y., 1883. Lives in New York.

117 **KUHN: Apples in the Hay.** 1932. 30 x 40 inches. The Museum of Modern Art, gift of Mrs. John D. Rockefeller, Jr.

Walt Kuhn. Born New York, 1880. Helped organize "Armory Show," New York, 1913. Lives in New York.

118 WATKINS: Boris Blai. 1938. 40 x 35 inches. The Museum of Modern Art, gift of A. Conger
Goodyear

Franklin C. Watkins. Born New York, 1894. Lives in Philadelphia.

119   DICKINSON: Plums on a Plate. 1926. 14 x 20¼ inches. The Museum of Modern Art, gift of Mrs. John D. Rockefeller, Jr.

Preston Dickinson. Born New York, 1891. Died in Spain, 1930.

120 **SPENCER: Near Avenue A.** 1933. 30¼ x 40¼ inches. The Museum of Modern Art, gift of Nelson Rockefeller

Niles Spencer. Born Pawtucket, R. I., 1893. Lives in New York. The work of Dickinson and Spencer has sometimes been termed "precisionist" because of their use of exact forms and sharp edges. Compare also Sheeler, no. 140, and Blume, no. 200.

121   ROUAULT: Head of Christ (Christ Flagellé). 1905. Oil on paper, 45 x 31 inches. Lent by Walter P. Chrysler, Jr., New York

Georges Rouault. French, born 1871. Lives in Paris. Influenced by Rembrandt, Daumier, Goya, and medieval stained glass, his work even when not specifically religious in subject matter is profoundly concerned with human injustice and pathos, subjects which he embodies in forms and colors of sombre power.

122   ROUAULT: Three Judges. 1913. 28 x 40 inches. Lent by the Lewisohn Collection, New York

EXPRESSIONISM

Rouault, although a Frenchman, is the greatest of the artists called "Expressionist," a term usually associated with German art. Expressionist paintings suggest an intense, even violent, emotional state which reveals itself in exaggerations and distortions of form and color, often with an emphasis upon pathos or melancholy. The work of van Gogh, nos. 68-73, Munch, no. 83, and Ensor, no. 82, was often Expressionist in quality as are the following works of Nolde, Kirchner, Beckmann and Weber. Soutine, no. 105, Kokoschka, no. 106, and Marin, no. 107, may also be called Expressionist. The distortions in Matisse's painting, *The Dance*, for instance, no. 91, are somewhat similar but they are primarily for decorative or dynamic effects.

123 **ROUAULT: Pierrot.** 1910. Oil and pastel on paper, 34 x 20 inches. Lent by Joseph Pulitzer, Jr., St. Louis

124 **WEBER: Invocation.** 1919. 47¾ x 42¼ inches. Lent by Mrs. Rose Gershwin, New York

Max Weber. American, born Russia, 1881. Studied with Matisse. Lives in Great Neck, N. Y. *Invocation* was formerly in the collection of the late George Gershwin.

125 NOLDE: Christ and the Children. 1909-1911. 34 x 41¾ inches. Lent by the Buchholz Gallery, New York

Emil Nolde. German, born Schleswig, 1867. Active in Germany until 1933. Allied before the War with the *Bridge* group of Expressionists in Dresden. His work is the richest in color and possibly the most deeply felt of any of the German Expressionists.

126　KIRCHNER: The Street. 1913. 46½ x 35 inches. Lent anonymously

Ernst Ludwig Kirchner. German, born 1880. Died Switzerland, 1938. Leader of
Bridge group, Dresden, 1905. His art is now officially forbidden in Germany.

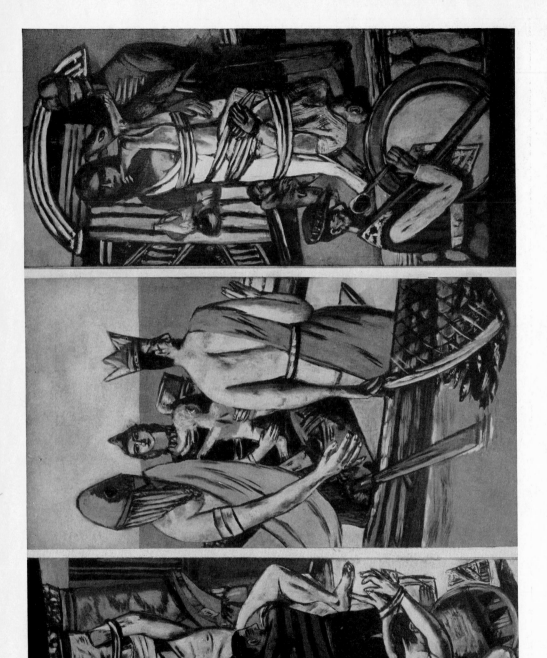

127 **BECKMANN: Departure.** 1937. Triptych: center panel 85 x 45 inches; side panels 85 x 39 inches. Lent by the Buchholz Gallery, New York

Max Beckmann. German, born 1884. Now lives in Amsterdam. One of the most powerful German Expressionists. *Departure* refers symbolically to his exile, caused by official disapproval of his art.

128 **GROPPER: Minorities.** 1939. 18 x 30 inches. Lent by the A. C. A. Gallery, New York

William Gropper. Born New York, 1897. One of the best painters among the politically conscious "social realists." Lives in New York.

129   MATTSON: Moonlit Still Life. 1938. 24 x 36 inches. Lent by the Frank K. M. Rehn Gallery, New York

Henry Mattson. American, born in Sweden, 1887. Lives in Woodstock, N. Y. One of the leaders of the American "romantic revival," inspired to some extent by the work of Ryder, nos. 26-29.

130 KANTOR: Provincetown Boat. 1937. 22 x 27 inches. Lent by John L. Sexton, Wilmington

Morris Kantor. American, born Russia, 1896. Lives in New York. His work is also romantic in feeling though less explicitly than Mattson's.

131   BERMAN: Winter. 1929. $36\frac{1}{8}$ x $28\frac{3}{4}$ inches. The Museum of Modern Art, gift of Richard Blow

Eugene Berman. Born Russia, 1899. Lives in Paris and New York. Endows his paintings of architecture with a feeling of "Neo-Romantic" mystery and melancholy. Compare Bérard's portrait, opposite, and Mattson, no. 129.

132 **BÉRARD: Portrait of a Man in Blue.** 1927. Oil on composition board, 39¼ x 28½ inches. Lent anonymously.

Christian Bérard. French, born 1902. Lives in Paris. The leading French master of the Neo-Romantic group which concerned itself, among other things, with an interest in psychological portraiture. The subject of this painting is a poet.

133 TCHELITCHEW: Sketch for *Phenomena*. 1938. 30 x 36 inches. Lent by the Julien Levy Gallery, New York

Pavel Tchelitchew. Born Russia, 1898. Works in Paris, London and New York.

With ambiguous irony the artist has painted himself, in the lower left-hand corner, as the only hale person in a world of freaks. This is a study for a much larger and more minutely painted canvas.

Phenomena and, in another way, Spencer's painting, opposite, are what would have been called "problem pictures" in the 19th century.

134　SPENCER: Christ Bearing the Cross. 1920. 60 x 56 inches. Lent by the Tate Gallery, London

Stanley Spencer. English, born 1892. Lives at Coockham-on-Thames, Berks. Has revived something of the spirit of the Pre-Raphaelites of the 1850's without, however, using their minute technique.

135 **STETTHEIMER: Margaret Burgess.** 1929. 38 x 20 inches. Lent by the artist

Florine Stettheimer. Born and lives in New York.

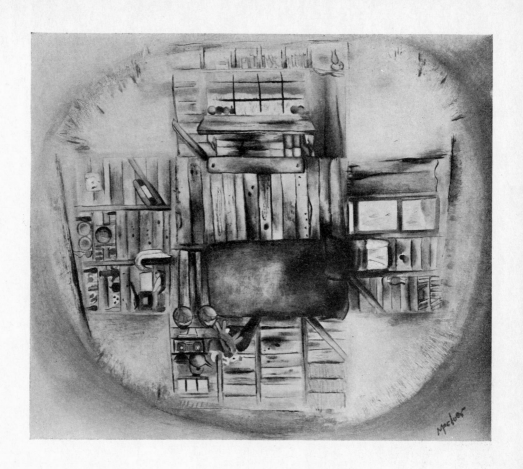

136 MacIVER: Shack. 1934. 20¼ x 24½ inches. The Museum of Modern Art, gift of Mrs. John D. Rockefeller, Jr.

Loren MacIver. Born New York, 1909. Lives in New York. The *Shack* is seen from above, the four walls opened out flat.

137 BELLOWS: Forty-two Kids. 1907. 42 x 60 inches. Lent by the Corcoran Gallery of Art, Washington

George Bellows. Born Columbus, Ohio, 1882; died New York, 1925. The most brilliant member of the group called "The Eight," some of whom shocked the public of 1910 by their bold technique and everyday subjects.

THE AMERICAN SCENE

The Bellows and the following paintings, nos. 137-149, are arranged in sequence because, however different in spirit and technique, they have conspicuously in common an interest in the American "scene," landscape, townscape, architecture, people, faces—in what seems specifically and characteristically American local color.

138   SLOAN: Pigeons. 1910. 26 x 32 inches. Lent by the Museum of Fine Arts, Boston

John Sloan. Born at Lock Haven, Pa., 1871. Member of radical pre-War group, "The Eight," which frequently used as subject matter commonplace scenes of American city life.

139   HOPPER: House by the Railroad. 1925. 24 x 29½ inches. The Museum of Modern Art, gift of Stephen C. Clark. *Illustrated in color portfolio II* (*see p. 379*)

Edward Hopper. Born Nyack, N. Y., 1882. Lives in New York. With Burchfield, helped make Americans aware of the picturesque dignity of late 19th century architecture.

140 **SHEELER: Classic Landscape.** 1931. 25 x 32¼ inches. Lent by Edsel Ford, Dearborn

Charles Sheeler. Born Philadelphia, 1883. Lives in Ridgefield, Conn.

141 **BENTON: Homestead.** 1934. Tempera on composition board, 25 x 34 inches. The Museum of Modern Art, gift of Marshall Field

Thomas Benton. Born Neosho, Mo., 1889. Lives in Missouri. Murals at New School for Social Research, New York (1930) were among the first to mark the rise of non-academic American mural painting.

142 BLUMENSCHEIN: Jury for Trial of a Sheepherder for Murder. 1936. 46¼ x 30 inches. The Museum of Modern Art, Mrs. John D. Rockefeller, Jr. Purchase Fund.

Ernest L. Blumenschein. Born Pittsburgh, 1874. Lives in Taos, N. M.

143   MARSH: High Yaller. 1934. Tempera on panel, 24 x 18⅛ inches. Lent by Mrs. John S. Sheppard, New York

Reginald Marsh. Born Paris, 1898, of American parents. Lives in New York.

144 **WOOD: Daughters of Revolution.** 1932. Oil on wood, 20 x 40 inches. Lent by Edward G. Robinson, Beverly Hills. *Illustrated in color portfolio II* (*see p. 379*)

Grant Wood. Born Anamosa, Iowa, 1892. Lives in Iowa City.

145 FIENE: Toward Evening, Pittsburgh. 1936-1937. 40 x 46 inches. Lent by Mrs. Edgar Kaufmann, Pittsburgh

Ernest Fiene. American, born Germany, 1894. Lives in New York.

146   LEVINE: The Feast of Pure Reason. 1937. 42 x 48 inches. Lent by the WPA Federal Art Project

Jack Levine. Born Boston, 1915. Lives in Boston.

147   HOGUE: Drouth Survivors. 1936. 30¼ x 48 inches. Lent by the Jeu de Paume Museum, Paris

Bought from *Trois Siècles d'Art aux Etats-Unis,* the recent Museum of Modern Art exhibition in Paris, by the Jeu de Paume Museum, a branch of the Louvre.

Alexandre Hogue. Born Memphis, Mo., 1898. Lives in Dallas, Texas.

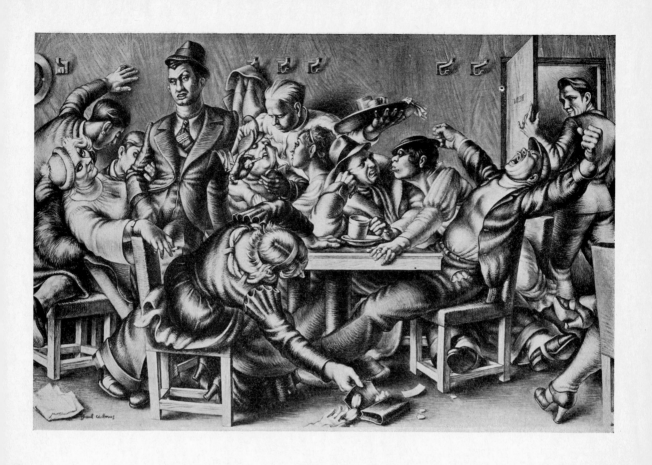

148 CADMUS: Greenwich Village Cafeteria. 1934. 25½ x 39½ inches. Lent anonymously

Paul Cadmus. Born New York, 1904. Lives in New York. The most merciless among the younger satirical realists.

149   MARTIN: Trouble in Frisco. 1938. 30 x 36 inches. The Museum of Modern Art, Mrs. John D. Rockefeller, Jr. Purchase Fund

Fletcher Martin. Born Palisades, Col., 1904. Lives in Los Angeles.

150 OROZCO: Zapatistas. 1931. 45 x 55 inches. The Museum of Modern Art, given anonymously. *Illustrated in color portfolio II (see p. 379)*

José Clemente Orozco. Mexican, born 1883. Murals in Mexico, Dartmouth College, and New School for Social Research, New York. Lives in Mexico.

The Zapatistas were the followers of Emiliano Zapata, the idealistic leader of the first *peon* revolution before the War.

MEXICAN PAINTING

The Mexican school of mural painting of which Rivera and Orozco are the most renowned, Siqueiros the most distinguished younger master, developed shortly after the War and has held its place as the foremost in the world. Both through its success in securing public walls to paint and through its achievement in making works of art out of social, political and historical subject matter, it has had an incalculable influence on painting in the United States. Rivera's *Fiesta in Tehuantepec* and Orozco's *Zapatistas*, though both canvases, are large enough to give some idea of the mural styles of the two leading masters of the school.

151 RIVERA: Fiesta in Tehuantepec. 1928. 79 x 64 inches. Lent by Mrs. James B. Murphy, New York

Diego Rivera. Mexican, born 1886. Murals in Mexico, San Francisco, Detroit, New York. Lives in Mexico City.

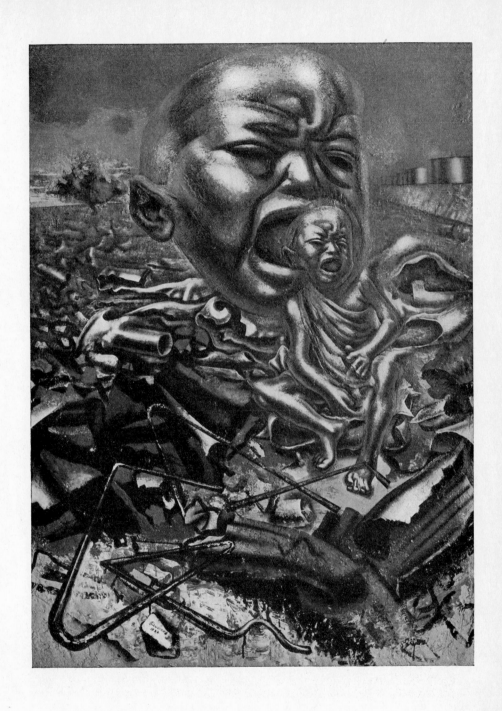

152 SIQUEIROS: Echo of a Scream. 1937. Duco on wood, 48 x 36 inches. Lent by Edward M. M. Warburg, New York

David Alfaro Siqueiros. Mexican, born 1894. Mural painter. Lives in Mexico.

152a   PORTINARI: Rio de Janeiro. 44½ x 57⅜ inches. Lent by the artist

Candido Portinari. Born at Brodowsky, Saɒ Paulo, Brazil, 1903. To Rio de Janeiro, 1916, to study art. Won scholarship to go to France, 1928. Now painting murals in Department of Education building, Rio de Janeiro.

153 PICASSO: Two Women at a Bar. 1902. 31½ x 36 inches. Lent by Walter P. Chrysler, Jr., New York

Pablo Picasso. Spanish, born 1881. To Paris, 1901, where he now lives. With Braque, founded Cubism (no. 157). For this reason he is placed at this position in the catalog though his incalculably protean art cannot be classified. His early work has greatly influenced the Neo-Romantic painters of 1930 (compare nos. 131, 132). His later work is claimed by the Surrealists.

During his early twenties Picasso passed rapidly through a number of phases. *Two Women at a Bar*, influenced somewhat by Toulouse-Lautrec, is characteristic of his Blue Period, in which the pervasive blue color intensifies the "blue" subject matter.

154 PICASSO: Youth. 1905. Gouache, 40 x 22½ inches. Lent by Edward M. M. Warburg, New York

155   PICASSO: Two Acrobats (Deux Saltimbanques au Chien). 1905. Gouache, 41½ x 29½ inches. Lent by the Thannhauser Gallery, Paris

After the Blue Period came a series of pathetic harlequins and acrobats, neurotically sensitive in technique.

156   PICASSO: Youth Leading a Horse. 1905. 86½ x 51¼ inches. Lent by William S. Paley, New York. *Illustrated in color portfolio I (see p. 378)*

Gradually, as in the *Youth Leading a Horse*, his work took on a stronger and more monumental character suggesting classical Greek art or, at times, Puvis de Chavannes.

157   PICASSO: Les Demoiselles d'Avignon. 1906-1907. 96 x 92 inches. The Museum of Modern Art, acquired through the Lillie P. Bliss Bequest.

In 1906 when Picasso was twenty, his gentle, almost sentimental art changed quickly into a storm center of audacious originality. He had studied El Greco's dynamic handling of light and the angular shifting planes of Cézanne's later style (as in the *Pines and Rocks*, no. 58). He was stimulated, too, by the arbitrary color and bold black outlines of Matisse and the "wild beasts" (*les Fauves*) of 1905 (see no. 91) and by the newly "discovered" barbaric masks of West Africa.

With this bizarre medley of sources in the back of his mind he worked for over a year on the extraordinary painting, *Les Demoiselles d'Avignon*. It was an imposing laboratory experiment which, more than any other single picture, marks a change in the direction of early 20th century painting. Studying the composition from left to right one can follow the metamorphosis which was to lead to Cubism and consequently to the worldwide tradition of angular abstract design. Like many transitional masterpieces *Les Demoiselles d'Avignon* is inconsistent and imperfect—but in no other painting has the most influential artist of our time expressed more powerfully his formidable and defiant genius.

158 PICASSO: The Poet. 1911. 51½ x 35¼ inches. Lent by George L. K. Morris, New York

For ten years after the *Demoiselles d'Avignon* Picasso and his colleagues concentrated upon Cubism, which from 1910 to 1912 became more and more "analytical." In *The Poet* the natural form is disintegrated into a composition of straight lines and overlapping planes leaving only a vestige of the figure's outline. In a spirit of ascetic research all decorative color was eliminated. (Compare Gris, no. 172)

159 PICASSO: Harlequin. 1918. 56 x 39½ inches. Lent by Paul Rosenberg, Paris

By 1915 Cubism had been transformed into a more decorative colorful style well illustrated
by this *Harlequin* of 1918, with his fiddle and sheet music, mask, tricorne hat and particolored
costume clearly recognizable, though broken up into a pattern of flat shifting semi-geometrical
planes.

160 **PICASSO: Woman in White.** 1923. 39 x 31½ inches. The Museum of Modern Art, the Lillie
P. Bliss Collection. *Reproduced, Museum of Modern Art Color Print No. 1 (See p. 380)*

Picasso, without abandoning Cubism, began during the War to paint some pictures in a more traditional style.
Of his "classic" period the *Woman in White* is one of the most charming works—a triumph of art over prettiness.

161 PICASSO: Seated Woman. 1927. 51½ x 38½ inches. The Museum of Modern Art, given anonymously

Almost exactly the same subject as the *Woman in White* but utterly different in character and spirit. As abstract as the *Harlequin* of 1918 but flowing curved lines instead of angular shapes are used to build the figure.

162   PICASSO: Portrait. 1938. 28½ x 24¼ inches. Lent by Walter P. Chrysler, Jr., New York

Though he has now been painting for nearly 45 years, Picasso's invention is unflagging and his color possibly more resonant than ever before.

163   PICASSO: The Mirror. 1932. 63¾ x 51¼ inches. The Museum of Modern Art, gift of Mrs. Simon Guggenheim. *Illustrated in color portfolio II (see p. 379)*

Like a medieval stained glass window in its glowing color and compact figures against an abstract lozenge-patterned background.

164 BRAQUE: Still Life. 1917. 25¼ x 36¼ inches. Lent by Joseph Pulitzer, Jr., St. Louis

A composition of roughly rectangular flat shapes varied by patterns and simulated textures (for the trick of *trompel'oeil* textures compare Harnett, no. 43).

165 BRAQUE: Still Life. 1929. 15¾ x 47¼ inches. Lent by Paul Rosenberg, Paris

166 BRAQUE: The Table (Le Guéridon). About 1928. 71 x 28¾ inches. Lent by Walter P. Chrysler, Jr., New York

Georges Braque. French, born 1881. Lives in Paris. The foremost French master of Cubism, which with Picasso he invented about 1908. He remains one of the most distinguished French painters.

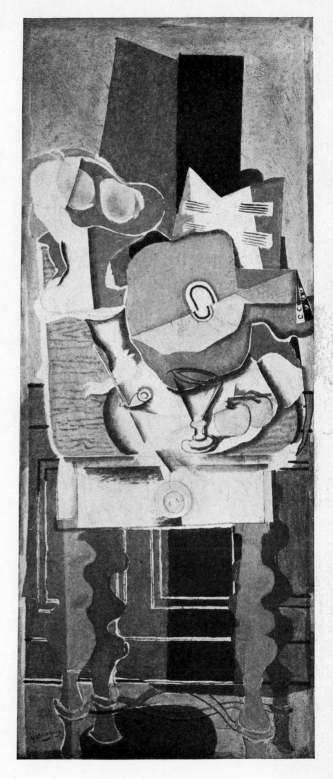

167 BRAQUE: Still Life. 1928. 20 x 36 inches. Lent by Frank Crowninshield, New York. *Illustrated in color portfolio II (see p. 379)*

168   BRAQUE: Painter and Model. 1939. 51 x 71 inches. Lent by Walter P. Chrysler, Jr., New York

169   LEGER: Under the Trees. 1913. 36½ x 29 inches. Lent by Walter P. Chrysler, Jr., New York

Fernand Léger. French, born 1881. Associated with Cubists, 1910-14. Courageously challenges in his art the brutal and clangorous rhythms of the machine age.

170 LEGER: Luncheon (Le Grand Déjeuner). 1921. 72¼ x 99 inches. Lent by Paul Rosenberg, Paris

Léger for many years has wanted above all to do mural paintings, hence the large size of these canvases.

171 **LEGER: Composition.** 1917-
1918. 98½ x 72¼ inches. Lent
by Mrs. Meric Callery, Boulogne-
sur-Seine

172   GRIS: The Sherry Bottle (Jerez de la Frontera). 1912. 28⅞ x 36⅜ inches. Lent by Walter P. Chrysler, Jr., New York

Juan Gris (José Gonzales). Spanish, 1887-1927. Worked in Paris; one of the foremost Cubists. Remarkable for the distinction and precision of his style.

173   GRIS: The Chessboard. 1917. Oil on wood, 28¾ x 39⅜ inches. The Museum of Modern Art, Mrs. John D. Rockefeller, Jr. Purchase Fund. *Illustrated in color portfolio II (see p. 379)*

174 LA FRESNAYE: The Conquest of the Air. 1913. 91½ x 77 inches. Lent by René Gaffé, Brussels

Roger de La Fresnaye. French, 1885-1925. Associated with Cubists. His rare large pictures are among the masterpieces of early 20th century painting.

175 FEININGER: Viaduct. 1920. 39⅝ x 33½ inches. Lent by the artist

Lyonel Feininger. Born New York, 1871. In Germany, 1887-1936. Professor at Bauhaus, 1919-1933. Lives in New York.

176 DUCHAMP: Young Man in a Train. 1912. Oil on cardboard, 39⅜ x 28⅝ inches. Lent by Walter Pach, New York

Marcel Duchamp. French, born 1887. Associated with Cubists, 1911; Dadaists, 1918; Surrealists, 1926. Lives in Paris. Painter of the famous *Nude Descending a Staircase*, to which the *Young Man in a Train* may be considered a companion-piece. Both are experiments in showing simultaneously successive aspects of forms in motion. Compare with Balla, opposite, and the *Golfer*, no. 378.

177   BALLA: Dog on Leash: 1912. 35⅝ x 43¼ inches. Lent by A. Conger Goodyear, New York

Giacomo Balla. Italian, born 1871. Lives in Rome. One of the 1910 Futurists who tried to paint forms in motion, anticipating such photographs as the *Golfer*, no. 378.

178 **DAVIS: Cape Ann Landscape.** 1938. 20 x 30 inches. Lent by the artist

Stuart Davis. Born Philadelphia, 1894. Lives in New York.

179 **STELLA: American Landscape.** 1929. 78 x 40 inches. Lent by the Jeu de Paume Museum, Paris. Courtesy Arthur F. Egner, Newark

Joseph Stella. American, born Italy. 1880. To America about 1896. Lives in New York.

179

180 KANDINSKY: The White Center. 1916. 47 x 53 inches. Lent by Maurice J. Speiser, Philadelphia

Wassily Kandinsky. Russian, born 1866. Founder of *Blue Rider* group, Munich, 1912. Professor at Bauhaus, 1922-1932. Lives in Paris. The first and most important of the abstract Expressionists who believed that painting should like music be independent of realistic subject matter.

181   MONDRIAN: Composition in Black, White and Red. 1936. 40¼ x 41 inches. The Museum of
Modern Art, gift of the Advisory Committee. *Illustrated also in color portfolio II* (*see p. 379*)

Piet Mondrian. Dutch, born 1872. Leader, *de Stijl* group, Leyden, 1917. Founder of Neo-Plasticism, 1917. Lives in Paris. Eliminating all subject matter he concentrates upon the division of the rectangular canvas into subordinate rectangles of white and pure colors, separated by black bars which are adjusted within a hair's breadth to achieve a perfection of proportion and balance. His art has influenced architecture and typography.

Both the Mondrian and Kandinsky are purely abstract, but otherwise they are almost opposite in character—the Mondrian precise, calculated, geometrical, classical; the Kandinsky comparatively amorphous in form and free and lyrical in arrangement as if improvised.

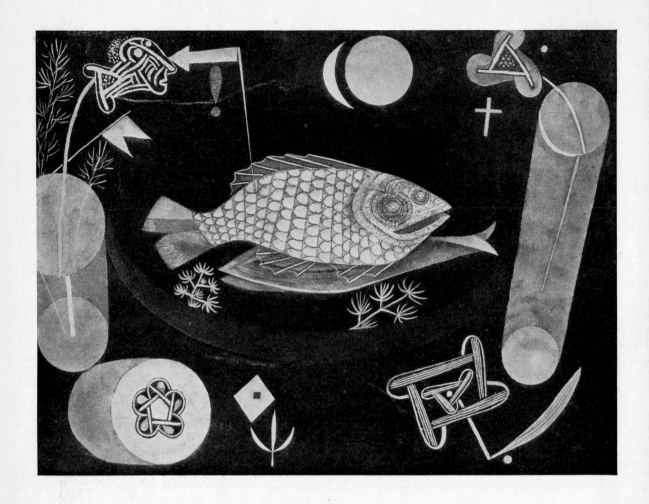

182 **KLEE: Around the Fish** (Um den Fisch). 1926. 18⅜ x 25⅛ inches. Lent anonymously

Paul Klee. Swiss, born 1879. Original member *Blue Rider* group, Munich, 1912. Professor, Bauhaus, 1920-1929. Switzerland since 1933. Under the influence of the art of children and primitive men, he paints fantasies of incalculable sophistication.

183 **KLEE: A Gay Repast** (Bunte Mahlzeit). 1928. 33¼ x 26¾ inches. Lent anonymously. *Illustrated in color portfolio II* (see p. 379)

FANTASTIC AND SURREALIST PAINTING

With the Klee begins a series of works, nos. 182-201, which may be roughly grouped under the heading of Fantastic or Surrealist. Some of the paintings are by men who participated in the Dada and Surrealist movements; others anticipated the work of these movements and still others, O'Keeffe and Blume, for instance, are quite independent in spirit, though in technique somewhat similar.

184 CHAGALL: I and the Village. 1911. 75 x 59¾ inches. Lent by René Gaffé, Brussels

Marc Chagall. Born Russia, 1887. Lives in Paris. Expresses native Russian-Jewish culture through the color and fantastic humor of his paintings.

185   de CHIRICO: Seer (Le Vaticinateur). 1915. 35¼ x 27¼ inches. Lent by James Thrall Soby, Farmington

Giorgio de Chirico. Italian, born in Greece, 1888. Lives in Florence and Paris. Twenty-five years ago, when abstract art was in its heyday, Chirico was exploring the romantic mysteries of dreamlike architecture.

Chirico's ominous lay figures pondering in airless perspectives anticipated the irrational fantasies of Surrealism. Compare Ernst, opposite, and Dali, no. 189.

186   de CHIRICO: Nostalgia of the Infinite. 1911. 53¼ x 25½ inches. The Museum of Modern Art, given anonymously. *Illustrated in color portfolio II (see p. 379)*

187   ERNST: Woman, Old Man and Flower. 1923. 38 x 51¼ inches. The Museum of Modern Art, given anonymously

Max Ernst. French, born in Germany, 1891. Dadaist, 1920; to Paris 1922; a pioneer of Surrealism, 1925.

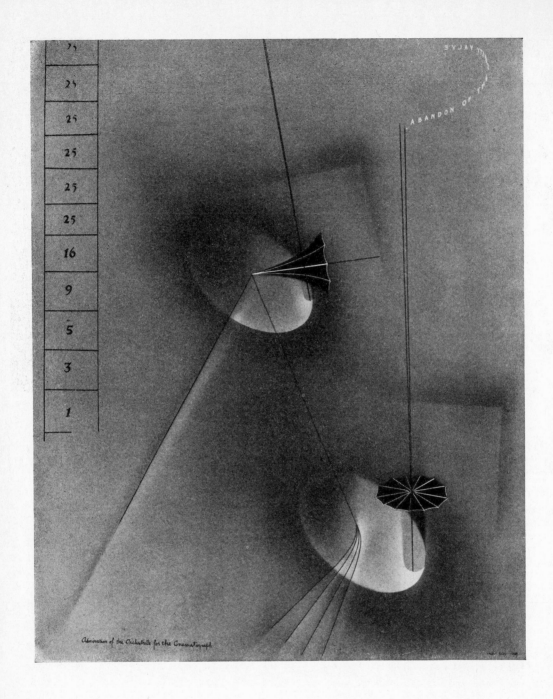

188 RAY: Admiration of the Orchestrelle for the Cinematograph. 1919. Airbrush, 26 x 21½ inches. The Museum of Modern Art, gift of A. Conger Goodyear

Man Ray. Born in Philadelphia, 1890. To Paris, 1921; Dadaist; Surrealist. Well known as a photographer (see nos. 366-373). Lives in Paris.

189 **DALI: The Persistence of Memory.** 1931. 10 x 14 inches. The Museum of Modern Art, given anonymously. *Reproduced in color on postcard (see p. 380)*

Salvador Dali. Catalan, born 1904. Lives in Paris. The *enfant térrible* of Surrealism. His *Persistence of Memory*, one of the most famous paintings in the United States, can according to the artist best be explained by psychoanalysis. He suggests that the flexible watches symbolize both the relativity of time and the artist's control over reality through art by bending even time to his will.

190 **DALI: Portrait of Gala.** 1935. Oil on wood, 12¾ x 10½ inches. The Museum of Modern Art, given anonymously. *Illustrated in color portfolio II (see p. 379)*

Gala Dali is the artist's wife.

192

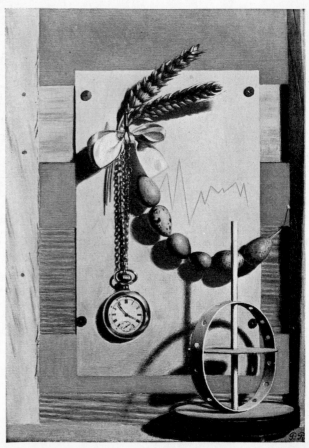

193   MAGRITTE: Mental Calculus. 1931. 26 x 45¾ inches. Lent anonymously

René Magritte. Belgian, born 1898. Associated with Surrealists. Before one's eyes the village of houses becomes a village of prisms and "perispheres."

194   MASSON: Battle of Fishes. 1927. Sandpaper, oil and pencil on canvas, 14⅛ x 28⅛ inches. The Museum of Modern Art, given anonymously

André Masson. French, born 1896. Associated with Surrealists. Lives in Paris. Uses a Surrealist technique, letting his hand move freely like that of a man absent-mindedly scribbling "doodles"; but Masson is an artist, so that the result is a work of art as well as material for psychoanalysis.

195 ARP: Mountain, Table, Anchors, Navel. 1925. Oil on cardboard, 29⅝ x 23½ inches. The Museum of Modern Art, given anonymously. *Illustrated also in color portfolio II (see p. 379)*

Hans Arp. French, born Strassburg, 1888. Dadaist in Zurich, 1916. Surrealist, 1925. Lives in Paris. The master of soft amoeba-like semi-abstract forms which have greatly influenced architecture and commercial art. See nos. 239, 319.

196 **MIRO: Personage Throwing a Stone at a Bird.** About 1926. 29 x 36¼ inches. The Museum of Modern Art, given anonymously

Joan Miro. Catalan, born 1893. Allied with Paris Surrealists, 1924. Lives in Paris. Remarkable for the complete spontaneity of his invention, his Surrealist sense of humor, and the excitement of his color.

197 **MIRO: Dialogue of Insects.** 1924-1925. 28¾ x 36¼ inches. Lent by Mme. Pierre Loeb, Paris. *Not illustrated*

198   DOVE: Nigger Go Fishin'. 19½ x 24 inches. Lent by the Phillips Memorial Gallery, Washington

Arthur G. Dove. Born Canandaigua, N. Y., 1880. Associated with the Alfred Stieglitz group. Lives at Geneva, N. Y.

199   O'KEEFFE: Red and Pink Rocks and Teeth. 1938. 20⅞ x 13 inches. Lent by An American Place, New York

Georgia O'Keeffe. Born at Sun Prairie, Wisconsin, 1887. Associated with the Alfred Stieglitz group. Lives in New York.

200 BLUME: Parade. 1930. 49¼ x 56⅜ inches. The Museum of Modern Art, gift of Mrs. John
D. Rockefeller, Jr. *Illustrated in color portfolio II* (*see p. 379*)

Peter Blume. American, born Russia, 1906. Lives in Connecticut. His subject suggests Surrealist paradox,
though he is independent of the Surrealist movement.

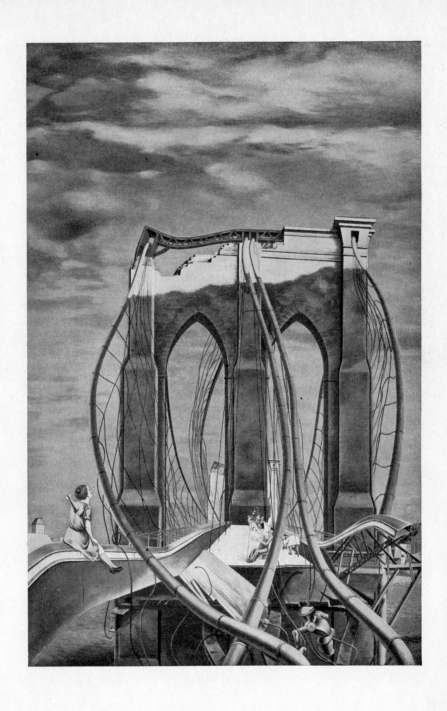

201   GUGLIELMI: Mental Geography. 1938. Oil on gesso panel, 36 x 24 inches. Lent by the Downtown Gallery, New York

O. Louis Guglielmi. American, born Italy, 1906. Influenced by Surrealists. Lives in New York.

202   **BOMBOIS: Before Entering the Ring.** 23⅝ x 28¾ inches. Lent by Mme. E. Hostettler, Berne. *Illustrated also in color portfolio II* (*see p. 379*)

Camille Bombois. French, born 1883. Lives near Paris. Formerly a wrestler and day-laborer, now one of the best self-taught painters. Compare Kane, nos. 1, 205, Peyronnet, no. 204, and the *Quilting Party*, no. 3.

MODERN "PRIMITIVES"

The Bombois and following three paintings by Bauchant, Peyronnet and Kane represent the work of a large number of artists who have had no professional training and have kept to some extent the naive innocent eye of the primitive **artist.** Most of them are artisans, tradesmen or laborers, men of the people, unsophisticated in technique, fresh in observation, untrammeled in imagination. The greatest of them was the 19th century Henri Rousseau (nos. 84, 85). Among the best Americans were Pickett (**no. 2**) and John Kane (**no. 1**).

203 BAUCHANT: The Treachery of Judas. 1933. 35⅛ x 46 inches. Lent by Mme. Jeanne Bucher, Paris

André Bauchant. French, born 1873. Lives near Tours. One of the finest colorists among modern self-taught "primitives."

Compare in subject the Stanley Spencer, no. 134.

204 PEYRONNET: The Ferryman of the Moselle. 35 x 45⅝ inches. Lent by Mme. Cécile Gregory, Paris

Dominique-Paul Peyronnet. French, born 1872. Lives in Paris. A self-taught "primitive." His picture illustrates a heroic incident in the Franco-Prussian War.

205 KANE: From My Studio Window. 1932. 22¼ x 34½ inches. Lent by Miss Adelaide M. De Groot, New York

John Kane is the best known modern American "primitive." For biographical notes see no. 1.
With the direct and simple art of John Kane this survey of modern oil painting ends, as it began.

AMERICAN WATERCOLORS

Watercolor painting is represented in this exhibition by the following group of twenty American works. There are many excellent European masters of this medium but, without undue patriotic prejudice, it may be said that probably no foreign 20th century school can bring together such a galaxy of watercolorists as Prendergast and Hart, Marin and Demuth, Burchfield and the recent welcome newcomer George Grosz.

206   **PRENDERGAST: The East River.** 1901. Watercolor, 13⅝ x 19⅝ inches. The Museum of Modern Art, gift of Mrs. John D. Rockefeller, Jr.

Maurice Prendergast. Born St. John's, Newfoundland, 1859. Died New York, 1924. His charming, decorative Impressionism is seen in his watercolors more purely if less sumptuously than in his oils. See no. 90.

207   **PRENDERGAST: Low Tide, Beachmont.** 1897. Watercolor, 17½ x 21½ inches. Lent by Charles Prendergast, Westport. *Not illustrated*

208   **PRENDERGAST: April Snow, Salem.** 1898. Watercolor, 14¾ x 21⅝ inches. The Museum of Modern Art, gift of Mrs. John D. Rockefeller, Jr. *Reproduced in color on postcard (see p. 380)*

209 **HART: Merry-Go-Round, Oaxaca, Mexico.** 1927. Watercolor, 17 x 23 inches. The Museum of Modern Art, gift of Mrs. John D. Rockefeller, Jr.

George Overbury ("Pop") Hart. Born Cairo, Ill., 1868. Painted in many countries. Died New York, 1933. His fluent technical virtuosity equaled his robust appetite for a wide range of visual experience.

210 **HART: The Mill Bousaada.** 1930. Watercolor, 17½ x 23½ inches. Lent by Mrs. John Parkinson, Jr., Westbury, N. Y. *Not illustrated*

211 **HART: Miami Beach.** 1931. Watercolor, 16⅛ x 24⅜ inches. Lent by Nelson Rockefeller, New York. *Not illustrated*

212 MARIN: Lower Manhattan. 1920. Watercolor, 21¼ x 26¼ inches. Lent by Philip Goodwin, New York

John Marin. Born Rutherford, N. J., 1870. Lives at Cliffside, N. J. The sudden flashing zigzag of his brush has by a repeated miracle of intuition produced a number of watercolors which place him, in the eyes of many, among the greatest American artists. See also his oil, no. 107.

213 MARIN: Autumn, Stonington, Maine. 1921. Watercolor, 19½ x 16 inches. Lent by An American Place, New York. *Not illustrated*

214 MARIN: Young Man of the Sea. Maine Series, 1934. Watercolor, 15½ x 20½ inches. Lent by Alfred Stieglitz, New York. *Not illustrated*

215   DEMUTH: Circus. 1919. Watercolor, 8 x 10⅝ inches. Lent by the Columbus Gallery of Fine Arts, Columbus, Ohio

Charles Demuth. Born Lancaster, Pa., 1883. Lived in Lancaster. Died 1935. The most exquisitely sensitive of modern American watercolorists.

216   DEMUTH: Illustration for *The Turn of the Screw*: "She had picked up a small flat piece of wood . . ." 1918. Watercolor, 8¹⁄₁₆ x 10 ⁵⁄₁₆ inches. Lent by Frank Calvin Osborn, Manchester, Vt. *Not illustrated*

217   DEMUTH: Acrobats. 1919. Watercolor, 13 x 7⅞ inches. The Museum of Modern Art, gift of Mrs. John D. Rockefeller, Jr. *Reproduced in color on postcard (see p. 380)*

218   DEMUTH: End of the Parade: Coatesville. 1920. Watercolor, 20 x 16 inches. Lent by Dr. and Mrs. William Carlos Williams, Rutherford, N. J. *Not illustrated*

219   DEMUTH: Fruit and Sunflowers. About 1924. Watercolor, 17⅞ x 11⅝ inches. Lent by the William Hayes Fogg Art Museum, Harvard University. *Not illustrated*

220 BURCHFIELD: Promenade. 1928. Watercolor, 32 x 42 inches. Lent by A. Conger Goodyear, New York

Charles Burchfield. Born Ashtabula Harbor, Ohio, 1893. Lives at Gardenville, N. Y. About 1918 he turned from a period of youthful fantasies to an equally original style in which the picturesque drabness of outmoded provincial streets and houses is presented with a curious mixture of hatred and sympathy.

221 BURCHFIELD: The Night Wind. 1918. Watercolor, 21¼ x 21¾ inches. Lent by A. Conger Goodyear, New York. *Illustrated in color portfolio II* *(see p. 379)*

222 BURCHFIELD: The Interurban Line. 1920. Watercolor, 14¾ x 20¾ inches. The Museum of Modern Art, gift of Mrs. John D. Rockefeller, Jr. *Not illustrated*

223   GROSZ: In the Park. 1933. Watercolor, 25 x 18 inches. Lent by Erich Cohn, New York

George Grosz. American, born Germany, 1893. Dadaist in Berlin, 1919. To America, 1932. Lives in Douglas-ton, N. Y. In America he has abandoned in large part the vitriolic caricatures which made him admired and hated in Germany, and has taken his place as one of our foremost watercolorists.

224   GROSZ: Chef. 1934. Watercolor, 23¾ x 17 inches. Lent by Erich Cohn, New York. *Not illustrated*

225   GROSZ: Punishment. 1934. Watercolor, 27½ x 20½ inches. The Museum of Modern Art, gift of Mr. and Mrs. Erich Cohn. *Not illustrated*

PAINTINGS BY CHILDREN
between the ages of 8 and 12 years

1877: an art critic

In a review of the Third Impressionist Exhibition, Paris, the critic of *La Chronique des Arts et des Curiosités* wrote: "Messrs. Claude Monet and Cézanne, happy to exhibit their work, have shown the first, 30 canvases, the second, 14. You have to see them to imagine what they are like. They make you laugh and at the same time are deplorable. They show the most profound ignorance of drawing, of composition, of color. When children amuse themselves with paper and colors, they do better." (Translated from R. H. Wilenski: *French Painting*, Boston, 1931, p. 242, footnote 2.)

c. 1895: Whistler

"On seeing at my shop the portrait of the *Sister of Cézanne*, which so strangely resembles an El Greco, Whistler said in all seriousness, 'If a child of ten had drawn that on his slate, his mother, if she were a good one, would have whipped him.'" (Translated from Ambroise Vollard: *Paul Cézanne*, Paris, Crès, 1924, p. 105.)

1913: Kenyon Cox (an American National Academician)

"Many of Matisse's paintings are simply the exaltation to a gallery of the drawings of a nasty boy." (Quoted by Walter Pach in *Ananias or the False Artist*, New York, 1928, p. 23.)

226 **Pauline Dublinsky,** age 10: **A Bowl of Fruit.** Gouache, 16⅞ x 23 inches. The Museum of Modern Art. Compare Matisse, no. 93.

227 **Jeane Hoisington,** age 11, Michigan: **A God of War Shooting Arrows to Protect the People.** Colored chalk, 18 x 24⅛ inches. The Museum of Modern Art

1928: John Marin (see his watercolor, no. 212)

"Taken from my own experience—I remember a certain day

looking at my paintings—my head began to swell—

it swelled enormously—came near killing me

a kid of six was the antidote—

with its little painting in colors in a book—

the cure was as bad as the disease—

my own head went down so fast

—it again—came near killing me—"

(John Marin: *A Few Notes* in *Twice A Year*, New York, 1939, no. 2, p. 177.)

1938: Aldous Huxley

"From an aesthetic and psychological point of view, the most startling thing about a collection of this kind is the fact that, when they are left to themselves, most children display astonishing artistic talents. . . . One can put the matter arithmetically and say that, up to the age of fourteen or thereabouts, at least fifty per cent of children are little geniuses in the field of pictorial art. After that, the ratio declines with enormous and accelerating rapidity until, by the time the children have become men and women, the proportion of geniuses is about one in a million. Where artistic sensibility is concerned, the majority of adults have grown, not up, but quite definitely down."

(From *They Still Draw Pictures*, The Spanish Child Welfare Association of America, New York, 1938.)

228   **Vera Baker,** age 8: **Yentas.** Gouache. The Museum of Modern Art

229   **Anthony Casale,** age 10: **The El.** Gouache. Lent by the WPA Federal Art Project

230   **Irving Gluck,** age 11: **City Houses.** Watercolor. Lent by the WPA Federal Art Project

231   **Barbara Kangile,** age 8: **At the Beach.** Gouache. Lent by the WPA Federal Art Project

232   **Fred Koops,** age 10: **Riveters.** Gouache. Lent by the WPA Federal Art Project

233   **Sebastian Lanotte,** age 9: **Deep Sea Diver.** Gouache. The Museum of Modern Art

234   **Donald Liguore,** age 10: **Going to Town.** Watercolor. The Museum of Modern Art

235   **Thomasina Pleasant,** age 9: **The Laundry.** Gouache. Lent by the WPA Federal Art Project

236   **Rhoda Rich,** age 12. **Dressmakers.** Gouache. The Museum of Modern Art

237   **Arthur Rosney,** age 12: **The Goldfish Bowl.** Gouache. Lent by the WPA Federal Art Project
The sculpture, no. 297a, and, if we can believe the artist, the painting, no. 86, were both done at the age of 15.

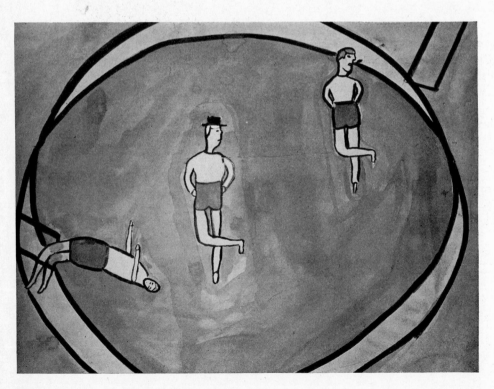

238   **Lena Safer,** age 12: **Flying Trapeze.** Gouache, 16¾ x 22 inches. The Museum of Modern Art. Compare Matisse, no. 91.

TWENTY-ONE PRINTS

The vast field of modern graphic art—drawings in various media, lithographs, etchings, woodcuts, book illustrations and posters, is represented in this exhibition by only twenty-one prints, though ten times this number would scarcely begin to cover the subject in any comprehensive way. Yet it is possible that this score of prints because of their special character may count more effectively in so large an exhibition than would a less concentrated number.

The twenty-one prints embrace a great variety of media and techniques, and most of the major points of view in modern art are represented by characteristic works. But the group as a whole is chosen with two special considerations in mind.

First: The great majority of the prints are by many of the foremost painters of the past fifty years for it is usually true that the greatest prints of any period are by the greatest artists rather than by the men whose reputations depend primarily upon their prints, however technically perfect these may be.

Second: The prints are deliberately chosen for their large size and bold character. Fine prints, especially etchings, are often so small or so delicate in technique that they are best seen in books or portfolios. But these twenty-one prints are large enough and strong enough to count positively as pictures on the wall. They can in fact compete with paintings—both in an exhibition and, more importantly, in the home. They show that a man—let us not call him a collector—can have for comparatively little money an original work by a great modern artist—a work, moreover, large enough in scale to count as the principal picture in his living room.

239   ARP: The Navel-bottle (Die Nabel-flasche). About 1922. 17½ x 13¾ inches. The Museum of Modern Art, given anonymously.
From *Arparden*, a folio of seven reproductions of drawings (about 1918) published by Merzverlag (Kurt Schwitters), Hanover. For notes on Arp see no. 195 and no. 319.

240 CEZANNE: The Bathers. 1899.
Color lithograph, 16¼ x 20¼
inches. The Museum of Modern
Art, the Lillie P. Bliss Collection

Cézanne's most important print. It is
based on a large composition of 20
years earlier now in the museum of the
Barnes Foundation, Merion, Pa.

**242 GAUGUIN: Women at the
River** (Auti te Pape). 1891-1893.
Woodcut, 8⅛ x 14 inches. Lent by
Mrs. John D. Rockefeller, Jr.

By boldly cutting and gouging his design directly in the plank Gauguin
freed the woodcut from its previous
servile role of reproducing drawings and
made of it an independent modern medium. Compare the woodcuts of Nolde,
no. 250, and Feininger, no. 251.

241 CASSATT: La Toilette. 1891. Color etching, 14 x 10½ inches. Lent by Mrs. John D. Rockefeller, Jr., New York

Like Degas, Manet and Toulouse-Lautrec who were her companions in the Paris Impressionist group, the American Mary Cassatt was strongly influenced by Japanese prints, especially in her etchings.

242

243 TOULOUSE-LAUTREC: Seated Clown (La Clownesse Assise: Mlle. Cha-u-ka-o). 1896.
Color lithograph, 20¼ x 15⅜ inches. Lent by the Marie Harriman Gallery, New York

From portfolio *Elles*. Also represented by the paintings, nos. 77, 78, 79.

244 MUNCH: Anxiety. 1896. Color lithograph, 16¼ x 15¼ inches. Lent by J. B. Neumann, New York

Like Toulouse-Lautrec, the great Norwegian artist, Edvard Munch, used a flowing and sinuous line which also appears in the *art nouveau* decorative design of the mid-1890's, but the disquieting atmosphere of his art is peculiarly his own. Compare no. 83.

245 VUILLARD: The Cook.
1899. Color lithograph, 13¾ x 10¾ inches. Lent by Mrs. John D. Rockefeller, Jr., New York

From series of twelve lithographs, *Paysages et Intérieurs*, published by Vollard, Paris, 1899. Compare his painting of about the same period, no. 88.

246 MATISSE: Reclining Nude. Lithograph, 17⅛ x 31½ inches. The Museum of Modern Art, gift of Mrs. Sadie A. May

Matisse once said that his lithographs, although published in many copies, should be more valued than his drawings, because they were so carefully studied. See also his paintings, nos. 91-96, and his sculpture, no. 303.

247   ROUAULT: Deposition. 1926. Process etching, 23 x 16½ inches. Lent anonymously

Rouault is also represented by three paintings, nos. 121-123.

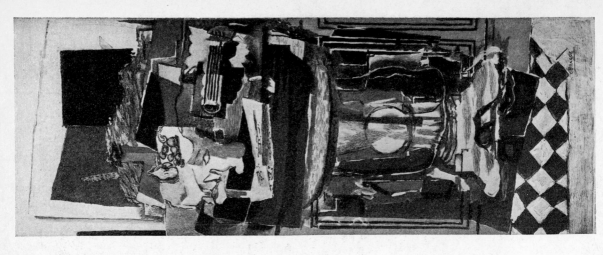

249 **VILLON** (after a painting by Braque): **The Table.** 1933. Color engraving, 23⅛ x 8½ inches. Lent by Mr. and Mrs. John W. Vandercook, New York

Jacques Villon. French painter and engraver, born 1875. Brother of Duchamp-Villon and Marcel Duchamp. Member of Cubist group, 1912. Has made a long series of color engravings after modern paintings. Lives near Paris.

248 **LEGER: Still Life.** Color lithograph, 21 x 17⅛ inches. Lent by Mrs. John D. Rockefeller, Jr., New York

Léger is also represented by three paintings, nos. 169-171.

251 FEININGER: The Gate. Woodcut, 16 x 17¾ inches. Lent by the Weyhe Gallery, New York

Lyonel Feininger, the American who recently returned after many years in Germany, is also represented by the painting, no. 175.

250 NOLDE: The Prophet. Woodcut, 12⅝ x 8⅞ inches. Lent by J. B. Neumann, New York

Emile Nolde, the German Expressionist, is also represented by a painting, no. 125.

253 KOKOSCHKA: Portrait, Ruth I. Lithograph, 27½ x 19¼ inches. Lent by the Weyhe Gallery, New York

Oskar Kokoschka, the Czech painter, is best known for his subtly characterized portraits. He is also represented by a landscape, no. 106.

252 KOLLWITZ: Death Takes the Children. 1935. Lithograph, 19½ x 16½ inches. Lent by the Buchholz Gallery, New York

Käthe Kollwitz, German, born 1867. First woman elected to Prussian Academy, 1918, but lost this position under the Third Reich. Lives in Berlin. Generally considered the greatest living woman graphic artist.

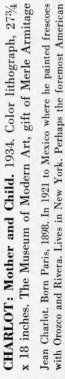

255 SIQUEIROS: Head of Saensz. Lithograph, 16¼ x 22 inches. Lent by the Weyhe Gallery, New York

See the painting, no. 152, for a note on the Mexican Siqueiros.

254 CHARLOT: Mother and Child. 1934. Color lithograph, 27¾ x 18 inches. The Museum of Modern Art, gift of Merle Armitage

Jean Charlot. Born Paris, 1898. In 1921 to Mexico where he painted frescoes with Orozco and Rivera. Lives in New York. Perhaps the foremost American master of color lithography.

256 **BELLOWS: A Stag at Sharkey's.** 1917. Lithograph, 18¾ x 24 inches. Lent by A. Conger Goodyear, New York

The most renowned American lithograph. George Bellows is also represented by the painting, no. 137.

257 **DEHN: Die Walküre.** 1930. Lithograph, 13⅜ x 17¾ inches. Lent by Mrs. John D. Rockefeller, Jr., New York

Adolf Dehn. American, born at Waterville, Minn., 1895. Lives in New York. One of the most brilliant American lithographers.

258 **GAG: Elevated Station.** 1926. Lithograph on zinc, 13⅜ x 15⅞ inches. Lent by the Weyhe Gallery, New York

Wanda Gag. Born at New Ulm, Minnesota, 1893. Lives at New Milford, N. J.

257

258

259 PICASSO: Minotauromachy. 1935. Etching, 19½ x 27¼ inches. Lent by Henry P. McIlhenny, Germantown

Picasso's most important print.

20TH CENTURY SCULPTURE AND CONSTRUCTIONS

As in the case of 20th century painting, 20th century sculpture is arranged without strongly emphasized divisions. At the beginning are the masters of more or less traditional technique and form, first those who are primarily concerned with modeling, then those interested in carving and chiseling. These are followed by the sculptors of the Cubist tradition, and the constructivists (nos. 313-314) and finally the sculptors of half-abstract, half-organic forms (nos. 315-323). There is of course a good deal of overlapping and the work of some men could be divided among two or three groups.

260 MAILLOL: Desire. Plaster, 47 x 45 inches. The Museum of Modern Art, gift of the sculptor

Aristide Maillol. French, born 1861. Lives in Paris. Something of the warmth and serenity of Greek sculpture is reborn in these works of one of the foremost living artists.

261　**MAILLOL: Torso.** 1910. Bronze, 43 inches high. The Museum of Modern Art, gift of A. Conger Goodyear

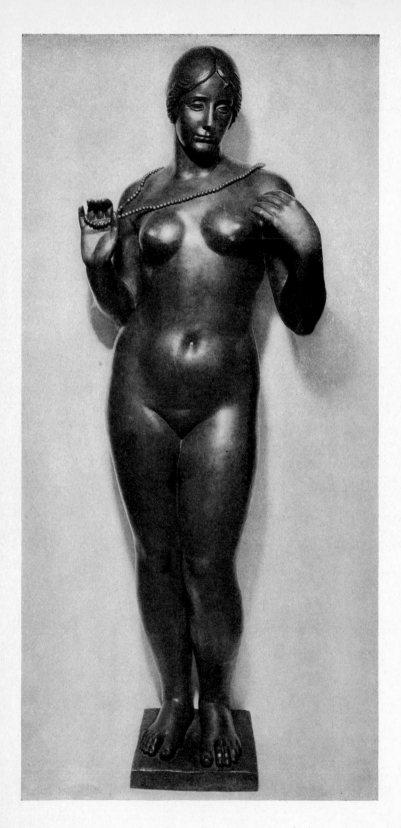

262 **MAILLOL: Venus.** Bronze, 69 inches high. Lent by the Brummer Gallery, New York

263 MAILLOL: Kneeling Woman: Monument to Debussy. Bronze, 36 inches high. Lent by A. Conger Goodyear, New York

264 MAILLOL: Head of Renoir. Bronze, 15 inches high. Lent by Mrs. Cornelius J. Sullivan, New York. *Not illustrated*

264a MAILLOL: Torso. Bronze, 34 inches high. Lent by A. Conger Goodyear, New York. *Not illustrated*

265   DESPIAU: Seated Youth. 1932? Bronze, 30 inches high. Lent by Mrs. John D. Rockefeller, Jr., New York

Charles Despiau. French, born 1874. Rodin's assistant, 1903. Lives in Paris. With Maillol, the most distinguished of the older generation of French sculptors. He differs from Maillol in his extremely sensitive surface modeling.

265a   DESPIAU: The Adolescent. 1929. Bronze, 46 inches high. Lent by the Weyhe Gallery, New York. *Not illustrated*

266 **DESPIAU: Assia.** 1938. Bronze, about life-size. The Museum of Modern Art, gift of Mrs. Simon Guggenheim

The most recent and possibly the finest of the artist's very few large figures. The reproduction is from a photograph of the original cast in plaster.

267 DESPIAU: Antoinette Schulte. 1935. Bronze, 18¾ inches high. Lent by Miss Antoinette Schulte, New York

Despiau is possibly the most acute of living portrait sculptors.

268 LEHMBRUCK: Standing Woman. 1910. Bronze, 76 inches high. The Museum of Modern Art, gift of Stephen C. Clark. *Not illustrated*

Wilhelm Lehmbruck. German, 1881-1919. One of the greatest of 20th century sculptors, much of his art is now officially repudiated in his own country. The *Standing Woman* is an early work under Maillol's influence.

269 LEHMBRUCK: Dancer. 1913-1914. Terra cotta, 11½ inches high. Lent by Nelson Rockefeller, New York

270 LEHMBRUCK: Kneeling Woman. 1911. Cast stone, 69½ inches high. Lent anonymously

Lehmbruck's finest work and one of the masterpieces of modern sculpture. Lehmbruck's mature work suggests the elongated elegance and spirituality of late Gothic sculpture.

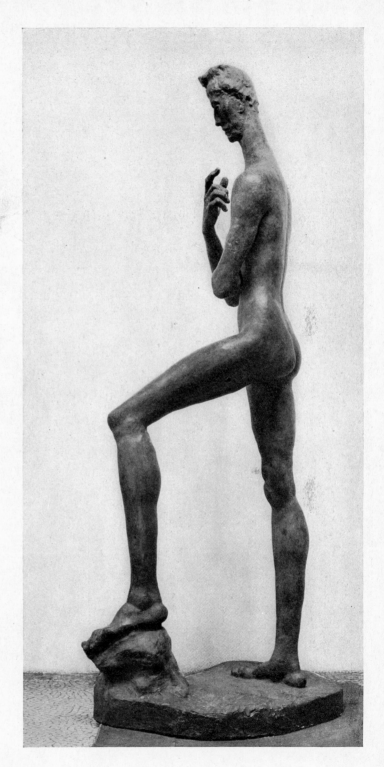

271 LEHMBRUCK: Standing Youth. 1913. Cast stone, 7 feet 8 inches high. Lent anonymously.

272   BARLACH: Singing Man. 1928. Bronze, 19½ inches high. Lent by the Buchholz Gallery, New York

Ernst Barlach. German, 1870-1938. Influenced by medieval and peasant sculpture and by van Gogh. His work is vehement or poignant in contrast to the impassive calm of much modern sculpture.

273   BARLACH: Head from War Monument, Güstrow Cathedral. 1927. Bronze, 14½ inches high. Lent by Edward M. M. Warburg, New York

274 KOLBE: Assunta. 1921. Bronze, 75 inches high. Lent by the Detroit Institute of Arts

George Kolbe. German, born 1877. Lives in Berlin.

275 KOLBE: Grief. 1921. Bronze, 15¾ inches high. The Museum of Modern Art, gift of Edward M. M. Warburg. *Not illustrated*

277

277 SINTENIS: Daphne. 1930. Bronze, 57½ inches high. Lent anonymously.

Renée Sintenis. German, born 1888. Best known for her small bronzes of animals.

276 KOLBE: Ascending Woman. Bronze, 62 inches high. Lent by the Buffalo Fine Arts Academy, Albright Art Gallery

278 MARCKS: Seated Girl. 1932. Bronze, 25 inches high. Lent by the Buchholz Gallery, New York

Gerhard Marcks. German, born 1889. Lives near Berlin.

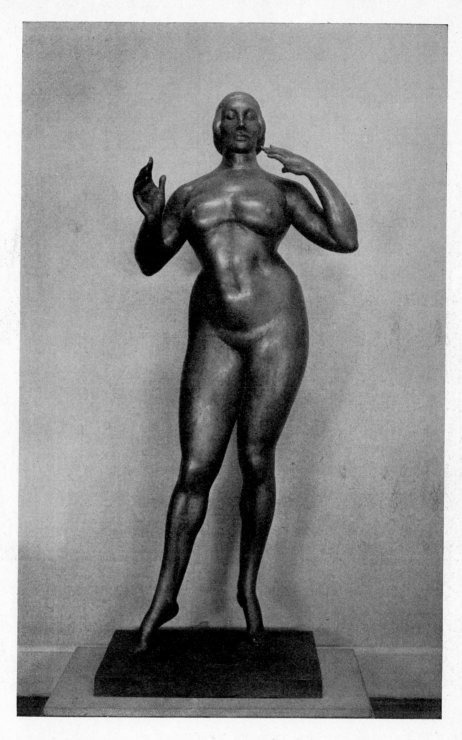

279 LACHAISE: Woman. 1912-1927. Bronze, 70 inches high. Lent by the Buffalo Fine Arts Academy, Albright Art Gallery

Gaston Lachaise. American, born Paris, 1882. Died New York, 1935. A master of the human form in its abundant and powerful maturity. Considered by his many admirers to be the greatest American sculptor.

280 LACHAISE: Floating Figure. 1927. Bronze (1935), 53 inches high. The Museum of Modern
Art, given anonymously

This, one of Lachaise's most original and important works, was given to the Museum by four of his admirers as
a memorial to the artist.

281 LACHAISE: John Marin. 1927. Bronze, 11 inches high. The Museum of Modern Art, gift of
Mrs. John D. Rockefeller, Jr. *Not illustrated*

282 LACHAISE: Man. 1930-1935. Bronze (1938), 8½ feet high. Lent by Walter P. Chrysler, Jr., New York

This, the first cast of Lachaise's largest figure, is placed ordinarily in the garden of Mr. Chrysler's house on Long Island. A second cast is shortly to be set in place near Mr. Nelson Rockefeller's country house.

283 EPSTEIN: Oriol Ross. 1932. Bronze, 25 inches high. The Museum of Modern Art, gift of Edward M. M. Warburg

Jacob Epstein. Born New York, 1880. Lives in London. Famous for his controversial figures in stone (*Christ, Rima, Eve*) and for his vigorous bronze portraits.

284 EPSTEIN: Mother and Child. 1913? Marble, 17¼ inches high. The Museum of Modern Art, gift of A. Conger Goodyear. *Not illustrated*

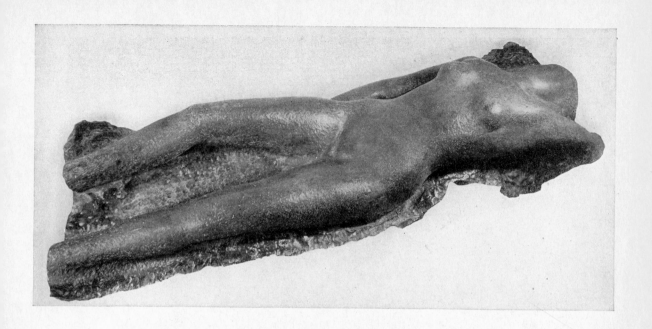

285 BAIZERMAN: Nana. 1938. Hammered copper, 96 inches long. Lent by the artist

Saul Baizerman. American, born Russia, 1889. Lives in New York. Uses *repoussé* technique, hammering out his fluid forms from thin sheets of metal.

286 JESPERS: Temptation of St. Anthony. 1934. Stone, 57 inches long. Lent by the artist

Oscar Jespers. Belgian, born 1887. Lives in Brussels. Contrast Jespers' archaic, rigid style with the more primitive but freer forms of Henry Moore's reclining figure, no. 321.

287 ZORACH: Child with Cat. 1926. Tennessee marble, 18 inches high. The Museum of Modern Art, gift of Mr. and Mrs. Samuel A. Lewisohn

William Zorach. American, born Russia, 1887. Lives in New York. Interested in cutting compact massive forms from stone and wood. His *Mother and Child* is generally considered a masterpiece of modern American sculpture.

288   ZORACH: Mother and Child. 1927-1930. Spanish marble, 66 inches high. Lent by the artist

289   ZORACH: Affection. 1933. Black marble, 30 inches high. Lent by the artist. *Not illustrated*

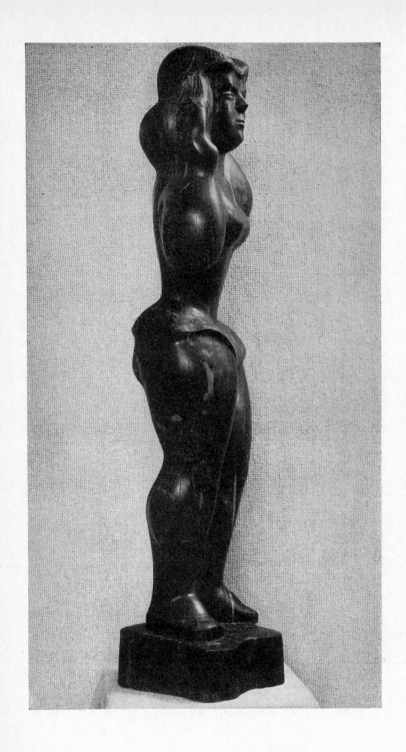

290   GROSS: Lillian Leitzel. 1938. Macassar ebony, 51 inches high. Lent by the artist

Chaim Gross. American, born Austria, 1904. Lives in New York. His figures reveal the qualities of carved wood, its smoothness and rich grain, as Flannagan's do those of hewn stone.

291 FLANNAGAN: Mother and Child. 1934. Red sandstone, 41 inches high. Lent by the William Hayes Fogg Art Museum, Harvard University

John B. Flannagan. Born Woburn, Mass., 1898. Lives in New York. He emphasizes the massiveness and rough-hewn solidity of stone.

292 FLANNAGAN: Triumph of the Egg. 1937. Granite, 12 inches high. The Museum of Modern Art, Mrs. John D. Rockefeller, Jr. Purchase Fund. *Not illustrated*

293 **WARNEKE: Wild Boars.** 1930-1931. Belgian granite, 20 inches high. Lent by the artist

Heinz Warneke. American, born Germany, 1895. Lives in New York.

294 **WARNEKE: Bear.** 1930-1931. Granite, 28 inches high. Lent by the artist. *Not illustrated*

295 LAURENT: Goose Fountain. 1931. Bronze, 41½ inches high. Lent by Mrs. David M. Milton, New York

Robert Laurent. American, born France, 1890. Lives in Brooklyn. His *Goose* shows what a good artist can do in the field of garden sculpture which is so often given over to banal prettiness.

296 HARKAVY: American Miner's Family. 1931. Bronze, 27 inches high. The Museum of Modern
Art, Mrs. John D. Rockefeller, Jr. Purchase Fund

Minna Harkavy. American, born Esthonia, 1895. Lives in New York.

297 **ROBUS: Girl Washing Her Hair.** 1933. Plaster, 17 inches high. Lent by the artist

Hugo Robus. Born Cleveland, Ohio, 1885. Lives in New York. Frequently embodies perverse humor in a stream-lined elegance of form.

297a **Mike MOSCO: Miner.** 1936. Bronze, 9¾ inches high. The Museum of Modern Art. Bronze cast, gift of A. Conger Goodyear. *Not illustrated*

Made by a 15 year old boy in a WPA art class in New York.

299 **BEN-SHMUEL: Pugilist.** 1929. Black granite, 21 inches high. The Museum of Modern Art, gift of Nelson Rockefeller

Ahron Ben-Shmuel. Born New York, 1903. Worked as a stone carver in Barre, Vermont. Lives in Pennsylvania.

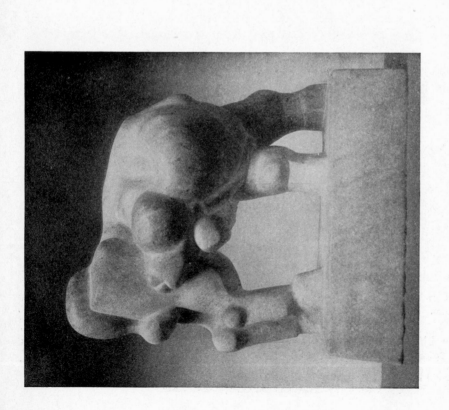

298 **NAKIAN: Young Calf.** 1929. Marble, 15¼ inches high. The Museum of Modern Art, Mrs. John D. Rockefeller, Jr. Purchase Fund

Reuben Nakian. Born College Point, N. Y., 1897. Lives on Staten Island, N. Y.

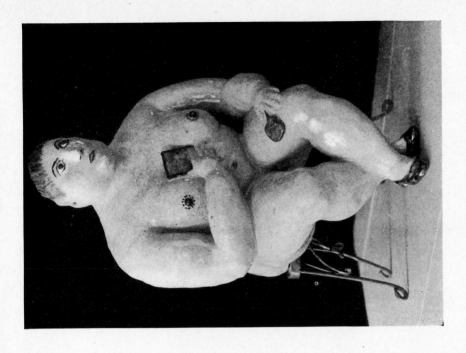

301 **WALTERS: Ella.** 1927. Ceramic, 17 inches high. Lent by the Downtown Gallery, New York

Carl Walters. Born Fort Madison, Iowa, 1883. Lives in Woodstock, N. Y. Combines a mastery of ceramic technique with a robust sense of humor.

300 **WHEELOCK: Meditation.** 1936. African walnut, 21 inches high. Lent by the artist

Warren Wheelock. American, born Sutton, Mass., 1880. Lives in New York.

302 MODIGLIANI: Head of a Woman. Stone, 26½ inches high. Lent by Mrs. Cornelius J. Sullivan, New York

Modigliani's stone heads done under the influence of African Negro sculpture are among his finest works, though less known than his painting, nos. 102-103.

304 PICASSO: Head. 1909.
Bronze, 16¼ inches high.
Lent by the Weyhe Gallery,
New York

A Cubist sculpture by the co-
founder of Cubist painting.

**303 MATISSE: Standing
Woman.** About 1914.
Bronze, 22¼ inches high.
Lent by Mrs. John D.
Rockefeller, Jr., New York

Henri-Matisse. French, born
1869. Though his painting is
far better known, Matisse has
at times been seriously concerned with sculpture. This
piece shows the influence of
Negro sculpture.

305   DUCHAMP-VILLON: The Lovers. 1913. Plaster relief, 27½ x 46 inches. The Museum of Modern Art, Mrs. John D. Rockefeller, Jr. Purchase Fund

Raymond Duchamp-Villon. French, born 1876. Influenced by the Cubists. Gassed in War, 1916; died 1918. Compare the *Lovers* with Maillol's *Desire*, no. 260.

306 DUCHAMP-VILLON: The Horse. 1914. Bronze, 40 inches high. The Museum of Modern Art, van Gogh Purchase Fund

The *Horse*, the sculptor's masterpiece, suggests a fusion of the forms and dynamics of an animal and a machine.

307 LAURENS: Seated Woman. Marble, 16 inches high. Lent by the Pierre Matisse Gallery,
New York

Henri Laurens. French, born 1885. Influenced by Cubists. Lives in Paris.

308 GONZALES: Head, 1936?
Wrought iron, 17¾ inches
high. The Museum of Modern Art, given anonymously

Julio Gonzales. Catalan, born
1881. Lives in Paris. Taught
Picasso technique of wrought
iron. His *Head* with its isolated
jaws and pronglike eyes is like
a far-fetched metaphor.

309 GARGALLO: Picador.
1928. Wrought iron, 9¾
inches high. The Museum
of Modern Art, gift of A.
Conger Goodyear

Pablo Gargallo. Spanish, born
1881. Died, 1934. Worked in
wrought iron, often using a
kind of witty shorthand in
suggesting form.

310   LIPCHITZ: Figure. 1926-1930. Bronze (1937), 85 inches high. The Museum of Modern Art, van Gogh Purchase Fund

311 LIPCHITZ: Pegasus.
1929. Bronze, 14½ inches high. Lent by T. Catesby Jones, New York

Although its technique suggests wrought metal the *Pegasus* is actually a unique cast.

Jacques Lipchitz: French, born Lithuania, 1891. Lives near Paris. Influenced by the Cubists and primitive art, he has become one of the most powerful, varied and original of living sculptors.

312 LIPCHITZ: Seated Man.
1925. Bronze, 22 inches high. Lent by Galerie Bucher-Myrbor, Paris

313   PEVSNER: Bust. Construction in metal and celluloid, 20⅞ x 23⅜ inches. The Museum of Modern Art, Mrs. John D. Rockefeller, Jr. Purchase Fund

Antoine Pevsner. Born Russia, 1886. Lives in Paris. With his brother, Gabo, founded Constructivism, Moscow, 1920. He believes that space defined by planes of glass or celluloid is a better material for art than solid masses of sculptured bronze or stone. Compare Gabo, opposite, and Calder, no. 325.

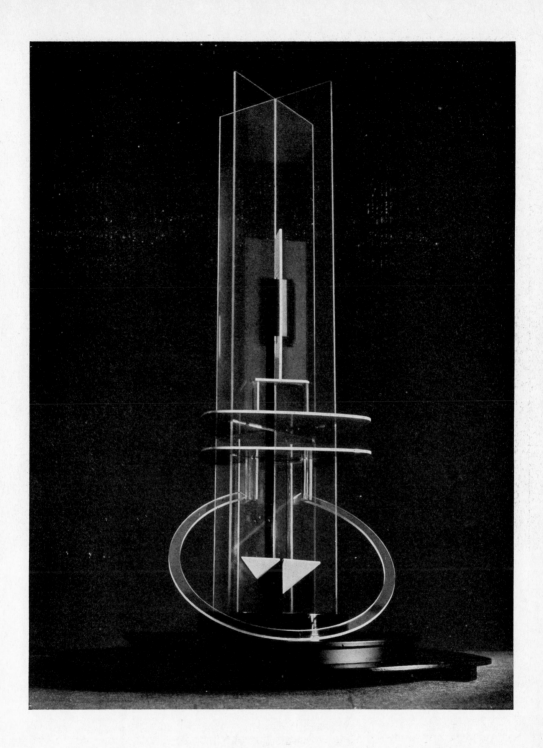

314 GABO: Column (space construction). 1923. Glass, etc., 41 inches high. Lent by the artist

Naum Gabo. Born Russia, 1890. Lives in London. With his brother, Pevsner, founded Constructivist movement, Moscow, 1920. The Constructivists combined a modern love of engineering technique with an interest
in space design.

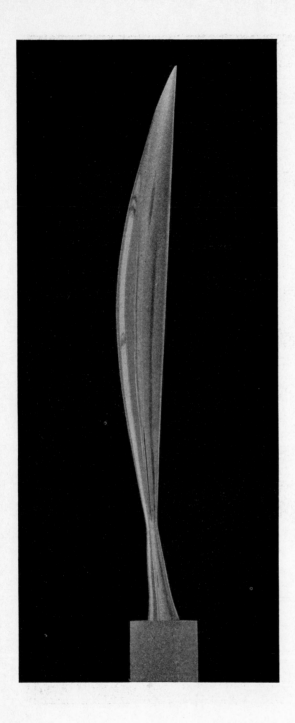

315 BRANCUSI: Bird in Space. 1919. Bronze, 54 inches high. The Museum of Modern Art, given anonymously

Constantin Brancusi. Rumanian, born 1876. Pupil of Rodin. Lives in Paris. The great sculptor of abstract forms which are beautiful in themselves rather than as representations of nature. In 1926 there was a lawsuit over his most admired work, *Bird in Space*, which the U. S. Customs held was not a work of art.

316 BRANCUSI: The Miracle. 1938. Marble, 60 inches long. Lent by the artist, courtesy the Brummer Gallery

317 GIACOMETTI: The Palace at 4 A. M. 1932-1933. Construction in wood, 25 inches high.
The Museum of Modern Art, given anonymously

Alberto Giacometti. Swiss, born 1901. Lives in Paris. Joined Surrealists about 1930.

318 GIACOMETTI: Young Girl. Plaster, 58 inches high. Lent by the Pierre Matisse Gallery, New York

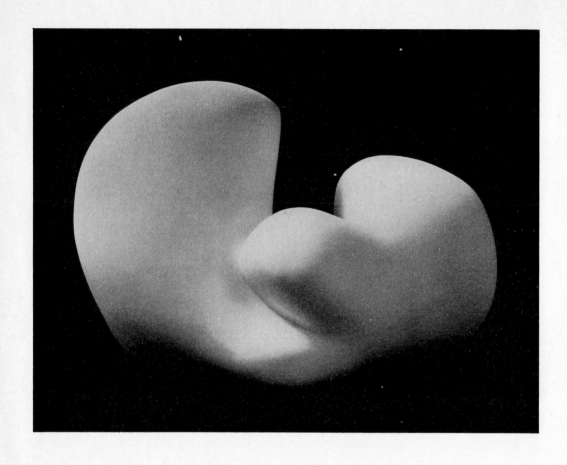

319   ARP: Human Concretion. 1935. Plaster, 19½ inches high. The Museum of Modern Art, gift of the Advisory Committee

Hans Arp. French, born Strassburg, 1888. Concerned with soft, organic forms in opposition to hard, angular character of the equally abstract Cubist style. Formerly member of Dadaist and Surrealist groups. Lives in Paris. Compare nos. 195, 322, 321.

320   MOORE: Reclining Figure. 1938. Lead, 13 inches long. Lent by the artist. *Not illustrated*

Henry Moore. English, born 1898. Lives in London. Foremost of the more experimental English sculptors.

321   MOORE: Reclining Figure. 1938. Hopton Wood stone, 36 inches long. Lent by the artist

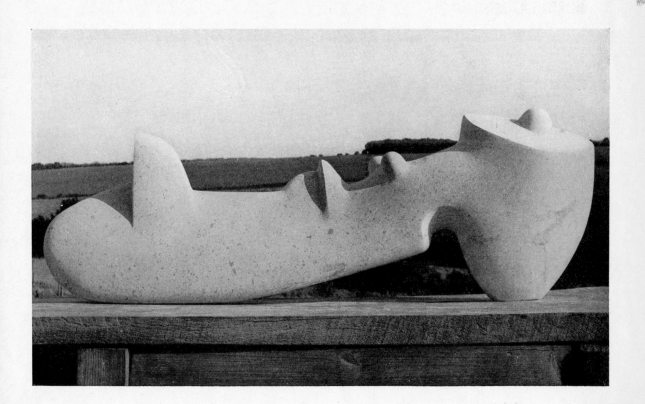

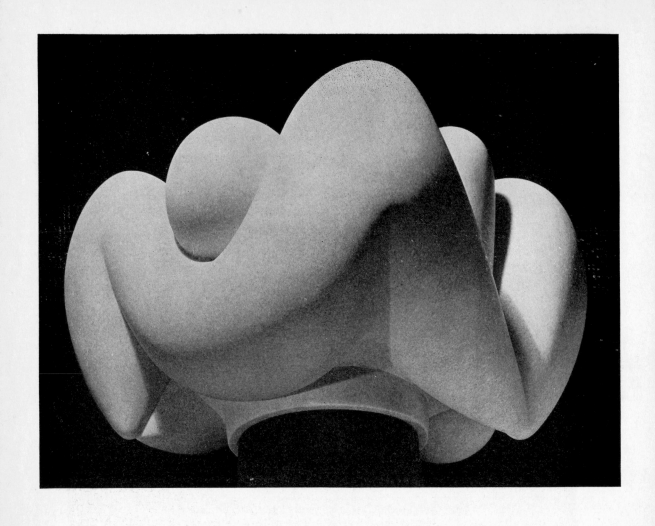

322 NOGUCHI: Capital. 1939. Georgia marble, 16 inches high. Lent by the artist

Architectural decoration, abandoned as superfluous for years past by the more advanced architects, now again is a possibility which Noguchi is anticipating in this capital. (Photo © F. S. Lincoln)

Isamu Noguchi. Born Los Angeles, 1904. Lives in New York. One of the most inventive younger American sculptors.

323 NOGUCHI: Miss Expanding Universe. 1931. Aluminum, 42 inches long. Lent by the artist

324 **FERREN: Composition.** 1936. Etching printed on plaster, carved and tinted, 9½ x 11¾ inches. Lent by Miss Louise Crane, New York

John Ferren. Born Pendleton, Ore., 1905. Until recently, lived in Paris.

323

325 CALDER: Mobile. 1935. Metal, 6 feet high. Lent by the artist

Alexander Calder. Born Philadelphia, 1898. Lives in New York. Internationally the best known of younger American artists. Combines abstract design with "Yankee ingenuity" and a sense of humor. His mobiles are especially interesting because they involve motion and continuous unpredictable change.

326 CALDER: Mobile. 1936. Cloth and wire. Lent by the artist. *Not illustrated*

Made originally as a banner for the old Museum building at the time of the exhibition of Cubism and Abstract Art.

SEVEN
AMERICAN PHOTOGRAPHERS

Ever since the daguerreotype process was first imported from France in 1839 there has been a tradition of straightforward photography in this country. The daguerreotype image, formed on the surface of a mirror-like silver plate, presents a wealth of detail that can be exhausted only by inspection through a magnifying glass. Even the fellow countrymen of Daguerre admitted that in America daguerreotypy found its greatest masters and its greatest popularity. The same mastery of brilliant detail we find in the Civil War photographs of Brady and Gardner as well as in the photographs of the Frontier taken in the 1870's.

When, toward the end of the last century, the invention of dry plate and film processes made photography a democratic medium, its simplicity summed up by the slogan "You press the button, we do the rest," the majority of artistically inclined photographers forsook the traditional straightforward approach. By the use of soft-focus lenses and other tricks they tried to make photographs resemble the painter's canvas or the etcher's proof, and so destroyed the camera's natural image.

Before the War, Stieglitz, Sheeler and Strand had already turned away from this style of photography, and returning to the older tradition had raised it to heights never before realized. Many younger workers began to follow their precision of technique and appreciation of the esthetic value of the unretouched and unmanipu-

lated product of the camera. The photographers in this exhibition took up photography in the 1920's. They all show a marked reaction against so-called "pictorial" or manipulated photographs, and have produced, by the direct use of the camera and by the exploitation of certain fundamentally photographic possibilities, some remarkable results. Although their approach is basically similar, their use of the medium is varied.

Ansel Adams delights in the extreme brilliance of a carefully made photograph. His western scenes are so lucid and detailed that, viewing them, our vision is extended and clarified until it becomes an esthetic experience. Even a cloud, as in *Thunderstorm, Lake Tahoe* (No. 353), has texture; the very atmosphere is registered on the film. He uses, whenever possible, large negatives and meticulous focusing to preserve the natural detail of the camera. But even when, for making exposures inconspicuously and rapidly, a miniature camera is employed there is no relaxation of the principle of rendering exact detail throughout the picture. The portrait of a New Mexican woman (No. 351) is an enlargement from the most striking of many negatives made in rapid succession. Such an approach demands an almost flawless technique.

Brett Weston, son of Edward Weston, shares with Adams a preference for "straight" photography. He has emphasized the power of the camera to reveal forms in an almost abstract manner. In

271

his *Broken Window* (No. 361) we are aware of the interesting shape of the black area before we grasp its identity. The isolation from its surroundings of a close-up view partially destroys the camera's illusionistic power, forcing us to observe immediately the relation of forms. Weston has used a variety of subjects in this way, but perhaps his most successful near-abstract photographs are those of sand dunes at Oceano (No. 365), where the lack of scale and the brilliant rendering of unexpected texture tend to postpone recognition of the subject while emphasizing the purely formal patterns of light and shade.

A somewhat similar use of the camera's revelation of abstract design is important in Ralph Steiner's work. His *American Rural Baroque* (No. 327) is an interesting composition. It is also, as its title suggests, interesting because of its subject. Unlike a painting or a drawing, a photograph implies at once the existence of the object which it represents. An unretouched photograph, with a richness of detail beyond the power of the human hand to render, emphasizes this realistic and seemingly objective character. Recently the value of photographs as documents, particularly of a sociological character, has been far more widely appreciated than ever before.

The photographs of New York which Berenice Abbott has been taking during the past few years are primarily documents of a changing metropolis. Yet they are by no means passive or unimaginative records. The skilful use of an abnormally thin format in her *Exchange Place* (No. 342) emphasizes the verticality of downtown Manhattan, and the strangely confused composition of freight cars, steamship and bridge (No. 348) is a vivid and accurate cross-section of New York's water front. This phase of her work continues, and extends, a tradition for documentation so ably carried on in France by Eugène Atget. At the time of his death Miss Abbott acquired his collection of negatives, and it is largely through her interest that Atget has been recognized in this country.

Walker Evans uses photography in a particularly sensitive way to comment upon our civilization. His choice of subject is eloquent, and his brilliant technique allows this subject-matter to be so readily grasped that the effect is often disquieting. In 1935 he helped outline the photographic policy of the Resettlement (now Farm Security) Administration.

Man Ray, who thinks of himself as a painter, has produced distinguished "straight" photographs (No. 373). He has also been most inventive in experimenting with various controls of the "straight" photograph. These controls are basically photographic, obtained by solarisation (partial reversal of a negative by exposure to light during development), by printing through various materials and other methods. His camera-less *Rayographs* are his most inventive works (No. 367). These are abstract or Surrealist designs created by the arrangement of objects on a sheet of sensitized paper which is exposed to light and developed. The outlines of the objects, their cast shadows and—when they are translucent —the degree to which they modulate light, are recorded in black, white and tones of gray.

Dr. Harold E. Edgerton is an engineer,

who developed high-speed photography as a scientific tool for the critical observation of rapidly moving machine parts. Using a high-voltage electric spark, whose duration can be accurately timed both for illumination and exposure control, he has been able to take photographs at one-millionth of a second. To use his own words, "Time is frozen and cut into pieces for exact examination." A series of these lightning-like exposures made on one plate traces mathematically the path of swift motion; the *Golfer* (No. 378), which bears such a striking resemblance to the much earlier futurist painting of Balla (No. 177), was made by this multiflash method. Dr. Edgerton has been quick to seize the creative significance of his work and has used his miraculous tool imaginatively and dramatically, so that his photographs even of commonplace movements often take on an astonishingly esthetic quality, revealing shapes and patterns hitherto unseen by the human eye.

BEAUMONT NEWHALL

273

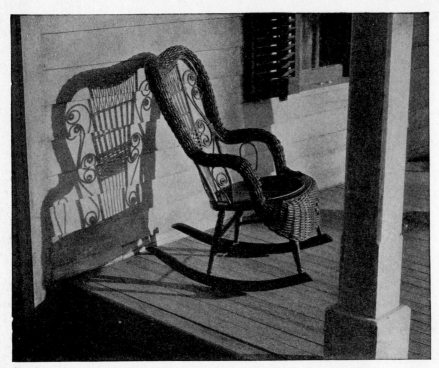

327

Ralph STEINER

Born 1899. Began photography, 1917. Now working exclusively with moving pictures. Founder of American Documentary Films, Inc.

327 **American Rural Baroque.** 1930
328 **Portrait of Henry Billings.** 1930
329 **Garage Wall.** c. 1930
330 **Suburban House.** c. 1930
331 **Trees.** c. 1930
332 **Model T Ford**—Detail. c. 1930
333 **Broadway and Exchange Place.** c. 1930
334 **Ventilators.** c. 1930

Lent by the photographer

328

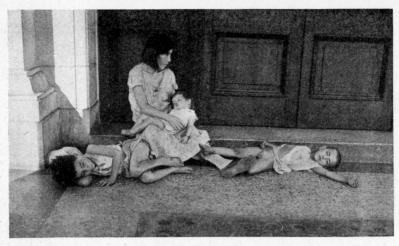

340

Walker EVANS

Born St. Louis, 1903. Began photography, 1928.
Now working in New York

Lent by the photographer, no. 340 from
Beals, Carleton, *The Crime of Cuba*,
J. B. Lippincott, 1934

Berenice ABBOTT

Born Springfield, Ohio, 1898. Began photography, 1924. Now working in New York

342 **Exchange Place, Manhattan.** July 1933

343 **Barclay Street Ferry,** from New York Telephone Building. July 1933

344 **Murray Hill Hotel: Spiral.** 112 Park Avenue, Manhattan. Nov. 19, 1935

345 **Newsstand,** Southwest Corner of 32nd Street and 3rd Avenue, Manhattan. Nov. 19, 1935

346 **Fifth Avenue, Nos. 4, 6, 8, Manhattan.** Mar. 6, 1936

347 **Portrait of José Clemente Orozco.** 1936

348 **Water Front,** from Pier 19, East River, Manhattan. Aug. 12, 1936

349 **Broadway to the Battery,** from Roof of Irving Trust Co. Building, One Wall Street, Manhattan. May 14, 1938

Lent by the photographer, nos. 344-346, 348, 349, courtesy of the Federal Art Project, Works Progress Administration

348

353

Ansel ADAMS

Born San Francisco, 1902. Began photography, 1927. Now working in Yosemite National Park

350 **Early California Gravestone.** 1935

351 **Old Woman at Coyote, New Mexico.** 1937

352 **Laguna Pueblo at Sunrise.** 1937

Lent by David H. McAlpin, Princeton, N. J.

353 **Thunderstorm, Lake Tahoe, California.** 1938

354 **Wrecking of Lurline Baths, San Francisco.** 1938

355 **Courthouse, Bridgeport, California.** 1938

The Museum of Modern Art, gift of Albert M. Bender

356 **Old Iron, Slag Pile, Colorado.** 1937

357 **Winter, Yosemite Valley.** 1939

Lent by the photographer, courtesy of David H. McAlpin

351

361

Brett WESTON

Born Los Angeles, 1911. Began photography in Mexico City under his father, Edward Weston, 1925. Now working in San Francisco

358 **Sand Dune.** 1934
359 **Sand Dune.** 1935
360 **Wood Erosion.** 1936
361 **Broken Window.** 1937
362 **Sand Dune.** 1937
363 **Wet Emery on Glass.** 1937
364 **San Francisco.** 1937
365 **Sand Dune.** 1938

The Museum of Modern Art, gift of Albert M. Bender

365

373

Man RAY

Painter and photographer. Born Philadelphia, 1890. Began photography, 1920. Now working in Paris

366 Rayograph. 1922
The Museum of Modern Art

367 Rayograph. 1922
368 Rayograph. 1922
369 Rayograph. 1927
370 Peach
371 Torso. 1923
372 Landscape. 1932
373 Portrait of Pablo Picasso. 1935

Lent by James Thrall Soby, Farmington, Conn.

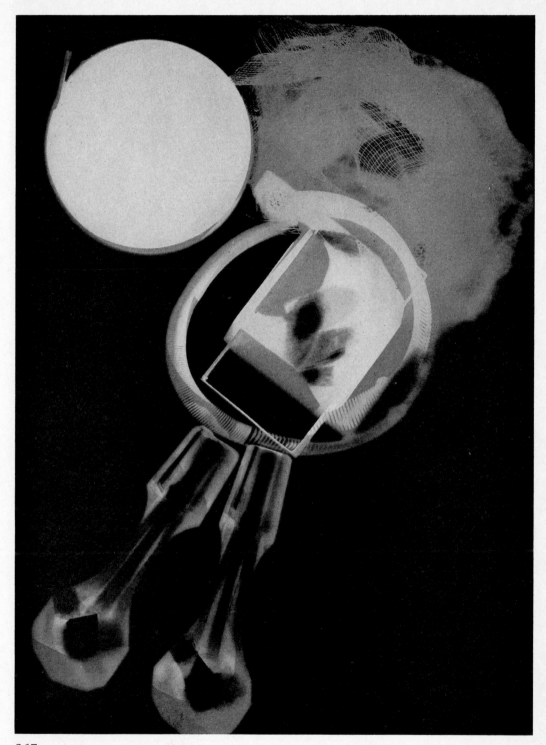

367

378

374

Frank Lloyd WRIGHT: Robie House. Chicago. 1908-9

Houses and Housing, the section of the exhibition which follows, has been organized in collaboration with the United States Housing Authority: Nathan Straus, *Administrator;* Catherine Bauer, *Director, Informational Service Division;* Frederick Gutheim, *Assistant Director, Informational Service Division;* Mary Cooke, *Designer.*

HOUSES AND HOUSING

No buildings are more important to a generation than those it lives in. The essential character of modern architectural design can be shown most vividly in dwellings built in the last ten or fifteen years—in houses, in apartments and in housing. This exhibition is intended to show the achievements of modern architecture in these fields.

THE MODERN HOUSE

Architects first developed a modern esthetic more consistently in the private house than in any other kind of building. Individual clients were more willing to experiment, or be experimented on, than speculative or commercial builders who were reluctant to take risks.

Relation between Function and Design

Two thousand years ago the Roman architect Vitruvius pointed out that good architecture must be built well, work well and look well. In modern architecture there is particular emphasis on the second. Construction, audacious and complex as it has become, is usually but a *means* of carrying out the demands of function.

In the twenties, many modern houses proclaimed their functional and structural honesty; good design was either ignored or supposed to result automatically as a sort of esthetic by-product. Le Corbusier said "the house is a machine to live in" (1921), but in his own work (page 294) we feel an artist's sensibility both liberating and disciplining his forms and even

guiding intuitively his choice of types of construction.

In the best work today it is clear that while design is *based* on functional considerations, it is not dominated by them. In choosing or inventing his forms and in arranging them, the modern architect is as free an artist as architects of the past have been. But it is its genesis in utilitarian forms which gives the style of a modern house much of its special character, distinct from houses of the past or today's imitations of houses of the past. For reference, a modern architect habitually consults manufacturers' catalogues while his neo-Colonial confrère is consulting picture-books of past achievements.

The Setting of the House:
Utilization of the Site

The form a house takes may be influenced by its environment, by the contours of the ground or by the direction of the view, the sunlight or prevailing winds. Thus, carefully proportioned as an interesting abstract shape in itself, Lubetkin's bungalow (page 296) is literally *aimed* like a camera at the superb view of the Bedfordshire meadows.

Adaptation to the setting is not only objective, but can have very real subjective values as well. No one has surpassed Frank Lloyd Wright in harmonizing architecture with its natural surroundings. Of one of his houses (see page 288) one could say that it seems "to have been born rather than built" far more appropriately

289

than Vasari did in eulogizing the 16th century Villa Farnesina.

The Plan of the House:
Utilization of Space

An important and characteristic innovation in modern architecture is the *open plan.* A generation ago, Wright was rethinking the house plan, discarding the traditional fitting together of rectangular rooms arbitrarily and irrevocably divided into space-boxes for special uses. He took his clients out of closed rooms and let them live in space, well organized in terms of efficient and pleasant living. This has been of tremendous influence on subsequent plan design. For example, in Miës' masterly Tugendhat plan (page 292) the living-space of the whole main floor is lightly subdivided by freely placed screen-walls; dining-, living- and music-rooms merge into one another. As a result the main floor is wonderfully spacious, for nothing is cut off nor shut away. The placing of these divisions is partly determined by function (the arc bounding the dining room is determined by the round table), but equally it is a subtle abstract composition, pleasing the spectator with a classically calculated balance of planes and, at the same time, a baroque series of changing perspectives and through-views.

Construction and Materials:
The Substance of the House

Today an architect can choose from a range of materials that would have dazzled his forbears. Modern architects of the 20's, aggressive in their modernity, scorned traditional-looking materials in favor of uncompromising flat stucco planes (pages 292-297). In recent, less puristic years wood, brick and stone have been restored to favor as we have come to notice the honest charm of straightforward regional building styles. Their reasonable use of materials with regard to purpose, cost and climate have been freshly and profitably seen and their natural affinity to modern building noted. In his unrivaled use of wood, Aalto owes more to "folk-architecture" than to orthodox modern clichés (page 299). The American wooden house has taken on varied modern forms (pages 300, 302, 305). Humble materials like cinder block, usually relegated to industrial building, have been legitimized (page 304). Unornamented, modern building has profited immeasurably from this new use of numerous materials, for their textures, often improved by exposure to the weather, enhance an unornamented style.

New types of construction also influence design. A light metal skeleton supporting floors and roof liberates walls from having to be placed where support is needed and permits great freedom in their arrangement (pages 292, 298). And walls which are used for support can be made in ingenious new ways, simplifying both construction and erection; they can be both thinner and cheaper than before and still carry their loads and keep out cold and heat. A whole house made at the factory is no impossibility as the scientifically studied Dymaxion scheme shows (page 307). Indeed, several completely pre-fabricated houses are already on the market. But it is improbable that these will suddenly replace the ordinary house. It seems, rather, that the latter is being *invaded* by pre-fabricated parts and pre-fabricated equipment—doors, windows and wall sections, heating, kitchen and

290

bathroom fixtures, and even whole bathroom units (page 334). Some good details originally designed for private clients have been taken over into mass-production and become available to any architect.

Pre-fabrication and standardization are having two main effects on design. First, the individual architect designs less and less detail because he can find wonderfully efficient and well made equipment in his catalogues. And second, standardized door, window and wall units introduce a regular rhythm. Expertly handled this regularity can become a virtue: and even in weaker hands it can still discipline design although it cannot keep it from being dull.

The Design of the House

But, technical conscientiousness and esthetic tact do not alone account for the special character of recent design. In the forming of most of his elements and in their disposition, the architect is guided but not tyrannized by necessity. He has many choices to make between solutions of equivalent usefulness and he has always some forms to design which are virtually unrestricted. A consistent esthetic discipline guides both his "functional" and free choices, harmonizing the forms and spaces he selects or invents.

Because architecture is an art and the modern architect a modern artist, his forms and colors are conditioned by the "cultural climate" he lives in. His forms are often an architectural embodiment of certain forms in contemporary painting and sculpture. The relation of Miës' plan (page 292) to geometrical abstract painting of *de Stijl* character (no. 181) has been pointed out. The fine organization of the ramps, wind screen and even the colors of the Savoye House roof-garden (page 295) parallel Le Corbusier's "purist" abstract pictures of the same years. More recently, as softly curved "organic" forms have become more important in abstract art, they have appeared increasingly in buildings (no. 319). The collaboration of Miro and Léger, Calder and Arp with Paul Nelson has resulted in a house (page 306) stylistically as homogeneous as Raphael's Villa Madama in which great Renaissance painters and architects worked together. The High Renaissance designer, perhaps believing that he had rediscovered ancient Roman architecture,[1] worked with a limited repertory of severely geometric forms and classicistic detail. The superb results match many of the major virtues of Renaissance painting and sculpture. The modern architect, often believed to be relentlessly "functional," works with a repertory largely derived from utilitarian forms, but at the same time his work is attuned to achievements in the other arts.

"Functionalism" is surely a word too restricted in meaning to describe modern architecture accurately. It may be a convenient name. ("Gothic" and "Renaissance" are equally inaccurate.)

[1] Renaissance Columbus thought he had discovered India.

Ludwig MIËS VAN DER ROHE:
Tugendhat House. Brno, Czechoslovakia. 1930

The street and its noises are shut out by the almost windowless façade. Milky glass walls enclose the stairway running down to the main floor.

The slender steel posts carrying the upper floor are frankly exposed; their orderly rhythm contrasts with the freely placed screen-walls which partially divide the main living space. New subdivisions can be made by pulling curtains along tracks on the ceiling. The 100-foot glass wall of the living-room sinks into the floor at the touch of a button.

The living-room and study are separated by a screen-wall of translucent onyx. Its vein-pattern and the reflections in its glossy surface make a luxurious piece of decoration. Modern architecture usually dispenses with ornament, and relies instead on the natural qualities of different materials (chromium-plated posts, glass, white ceiling, gray linoleum floor, honey-colored onyx and dark red macassar ebony of curved dining-room wall).

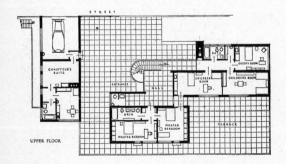

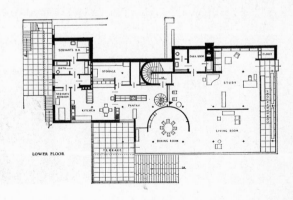

LE CORBUSIER and JEANNERET:
Savoye House. Poissy-sur-Seine, France, 1929-30

The main floor is one flight up, for the French do not like to live on the ground floor.

The route of a car being driven to the garage determines the curve bounding the ground floor.

The rooms of the main floor, conveniently arranged in relation to each other, all fit into a simple rectangle. Included as an extra room is an unroofed terrace, separated from the living-room only by sliding glass doors. The windows of the living-room are continued along the terrace as glassless openings in the wall, regularizing the design.

A ramp leads to the flat roof where the occupants exercise and sun-bathe. The rose and blue curving wind-shelter makes a subtle contrast in color and shape with the severity of the buff block below.

294

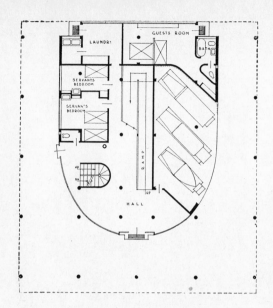

Ground floor

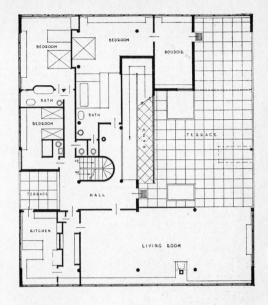

Main floor

Model of terrace and roof garden

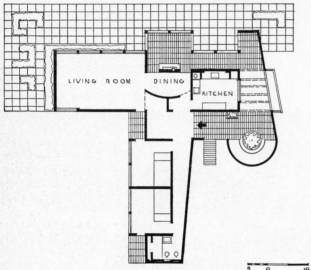

LIVING ROOM   DINING   KITCHEN

5   0   10

LUBETKIN and TECTON:
Bungalow for B. Lubetkin. Whipsnade, Bedfordshire, England. 1935

The architect designed this house for himself; with a personal quality rare in modern architecture. For week-end use only, it is much more open than would ordinarily be possible. Meals are served in the sheltered loggia—a sort of outdoor living-room with flowering plants and a fishpond. Each bedroom has its own sleeping-porch.

Alvar and Aino AALTO: "Mairea," Gullichsen House, near
Pori, Finland. 1938-39

(**1**) Entry; (**2**) Hall; (**3**) Living-room; usually subdivided by movable partitions. In these partitions is stored a collection of modern paintings only a
changing half dozen of which is hung at one time. (**4**) Reading alcove,
temporarily separated from living-room by three lengths of movable wall.
(**5**) Conservatory; (**6**) Dining-room; (**7**) Office; (**8-9**) Pantry & Kitchen;
(**10, 11, 12**) Servants' quarters.

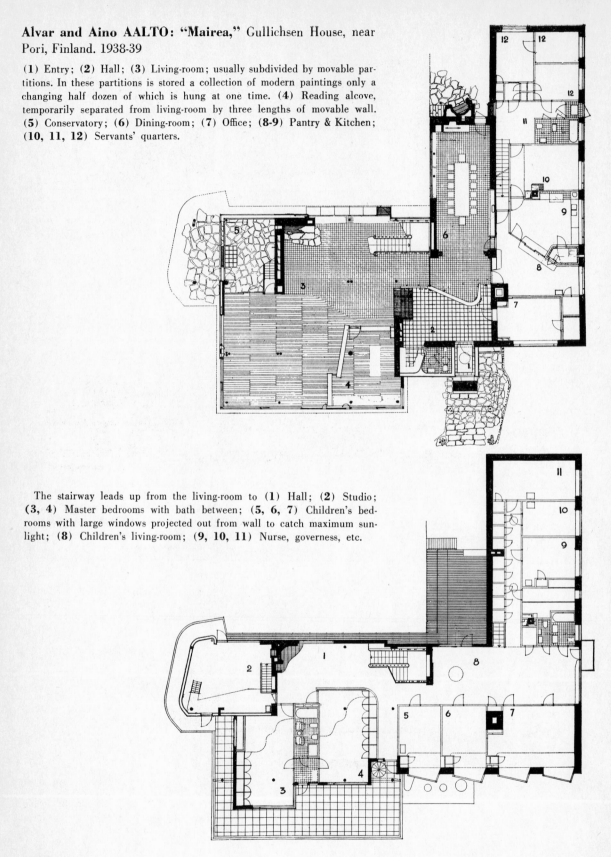

The stairway leads up from the living-room to (**1**) Hall; (**2**) Studio;
(**3, 4**) Master bedrooms with bath between; (**5, 6, 7**) Children's bedrooms with large windows projected out from wall to catch maximum sunlight; (**8**) Children's living-room; (**9, 10, 11**) Nurse, governess, etc.

298

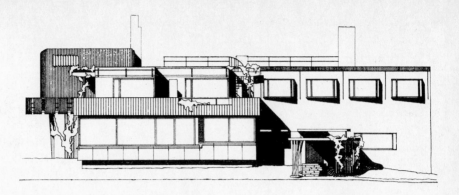

South elevation: The entrance is under the wooden porch at the right. The wall below the large living-room windows at the left is faced with slabs of black stone, the balcony above with planks of teak.

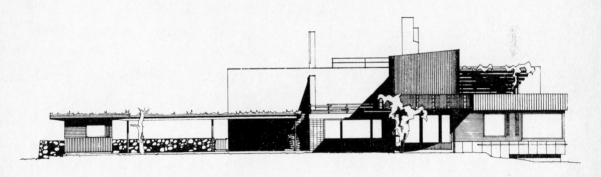

East elevation: The log cabin at the left is a Finnish steam-bath, standing on the edge of a large swimming pool. A connecting loggia, with flowering grasses growing on its roof runs to the main building. Studio and master bedrooms (upper right) open on a vine-shaded balcony.

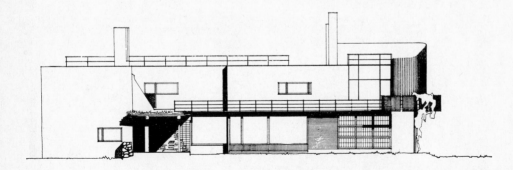

North elevation: Few windows pierce the white brick wall on the north side of the house. Only the living-room windows are large, and these are sheltered by the projecting service wing.

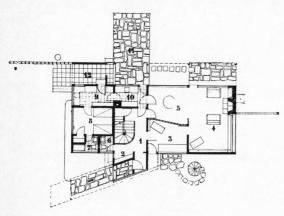

**Walter GROPIUS and Marcel BREUER:
Gropius House.** Lincoln, Mass. 1938

The sun-screen projecting horizontally beyond the eaves
(upper left) is placed with astronomical precision. In
summer it shades the living-room windows below; in winter, when the path of the sun is lower, its shadow falls on
the blank wall, and the living-room is flooded with sun-
shine. (photo Davis)

First floor plan: (**1**) Entry; (**2**) Coats; (**3**) Study;
(**4**) Living-room; (**5**) Dining-room; (**8**) Maid's room
and bath; (**9, 10**) Kitchen and pantry

→

Second floor plan: (**4**) Dressing-room; (**5**) Master
bedroom; (**6**) Guest room; (**7**) Child's room; (**8**) Bed
alcove; (**9**) Open roof deck; (**10**) Sewing room

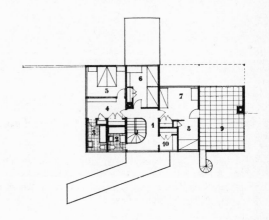

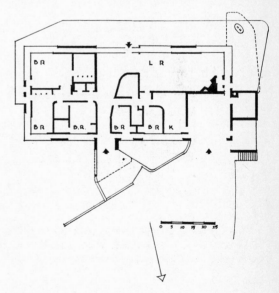

William LESCAZE: Loomis House. Tuxedo
Park, N. Y. 1937-38

A two-foot air space separates the inner and outer shells
of this "house within a house" and permits unusual precision in air-conditioning, a special interest of the scien-
tist-owner. (photo Ralph Steiner)

Frank Lloyd WRIGHT: Jacobs House:
Madison, Wisconsin. 1937

This small house demonstrates Wright's technical ingenuity and sound planning.

L-shaped, it shuts off the street and guarantees privacy for the small garden it cloisters.

The walls, only 2½″ thick, are built up of three layers of wood screwed together with building paper between. The outside and inside facing is of pine and redwood boards; the core is plywood. The flat roof is formed of three layers of 2 x 4's.

The heating comes from pipes incorporated in the concrete floor slab. The warm floor and the exceptional insulating properties of walls and roof mean that the house is uniformly comfortable at ten to fifteen degrees lower temperature than usual.

Not only inexpensive to build (exactly $5,500 including architect's fee) the house is also inexpensive to operate. (photo Petersen)

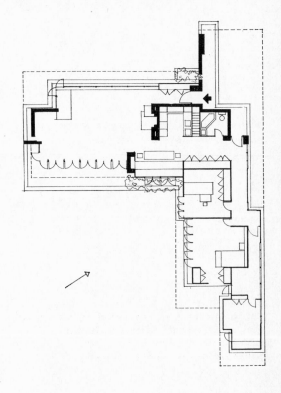

Richard J. NEUTRA:
Superplywood Model House. West-
wood, Cal. 1936

This $8,000 vacation house has been in-
geniously designed so that it can be taken
down, transported, and re-erected elsewhere
on simple new foundations. The walls are
made in sections of the same width as the
standard aluminum strips covering the joints;
on the inside, the walls are faced with
Philippine mahogany or painted cloth.

Throughout it makes use of standardized
parts and stock equipment to a degree that
suggests that the whole house would be suit-
able for modified pre-fabrication. Mass-production of the different elements would, of
course, reduce cost. (photo Luckhaus)

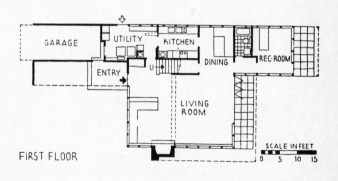

FIRST FLOOR

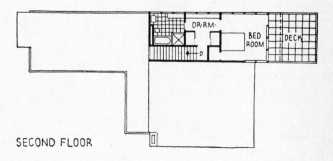

SECOND FLOOR

303

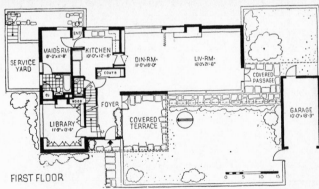

FIRST FLOOR

Edward D. STONE and Carl S. KOCH, Jr.: Koch House. Cambridge, Mass. 1938

Almost every inch of the small corner lot is utilized, for the two shady walled gardens are secluded enough to use as living-rooms in pleasant weather. The native stone walls differentiate the gardens from the house with its walls of painted cinder-block.

Each of the bedrooms on the compact second floor has good cross-ventilation. (photo Stoller)

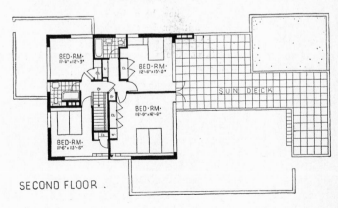

SECOND FLOOR .

304

J. B. Yeon, A. E. Doyle and Associates: Watzek House. Portland, Oregon. 1938

Modern houses often have much more in common with straightforward native building types than with the historical "styles." This house is emphatically American, and, without being derivative, it fits easily into our unsung tradition of plain and honest building.

The quiet sweep of simple forms harmoniously complements the fine Western landscape. (photo Boychuk)

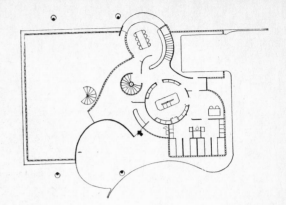

Paul NELSON: Model for a "Suspended House." 1938. The Museum of Modern Art, gift of the Advisory Committee

The rooms are suspended from the roof which is supported by two steel arches. These span the box-like outer shell of translucent glass. The free forms of the rooms within are possible with suspended construction and sheet metal walls.

The mural paintings are by Léger and Miro, the sculpture in this photograph by Arp. (The sculpture in the model on exhibition is by Calder.)

Ground floor (above): Large living-room at left. Oval dining-room. Round kitchen in center. Servants' rooms lower right.

Second floor (right): Reached by 2 circular stairways. Living-room balcony leads to terrace on roof of servants' group. Round library and 2 ovoid studies. A winding ramp leads on up to the bedrooms.

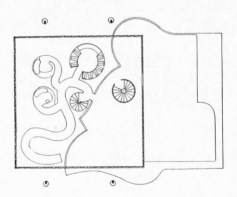

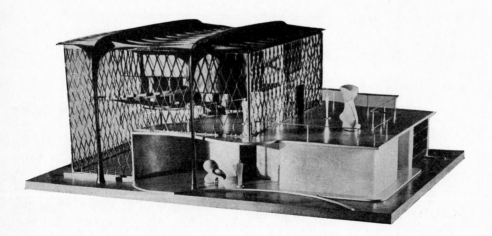

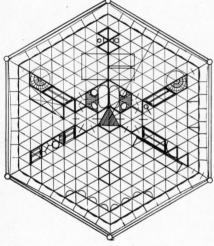

Buckminster FULLER: Model for a "Dymaxion House." 1927

An experimental house, conceived as a regular mass-produced commodity (like an automobile) delivered and erected by the manufacturer in one day.

The tubular metal chassis is suspended by steel guys from a central mast containing elevator and all services. Fresh air is drawn through a "nostril" at the top.

MULTIPLE DWELLINGS

The Apartment House

More people live in apartments every year since through sharing heating, electricity, walls and service families can enjoy more benefits for less money. The requirements for one family are essentially the same whether they live in an apartment or in a house, but the architectural solution is different. The apartment house is not an enlargement of the house either in plan or elevation; it is more like a compact multiplication of it.

The individual apartment cannot ordinarily be tailored to fit special personal preferences as can the individual house; it must be designed to meet typical and generalized needs. Each apartment becomes the unit of design and it must be standardized sufficiently to benefit both economically and esthetically from repetition. Europe remains far ahead of America in modern apartment design. We excel only in bathrooms and compact kitchens.

Clustered, apartments have fewer outside walls than houses so that it is more difficult to insure adequate light and air. The Highpoint apartment house in London takes the form of a double cross (page 309) with each arm only one apartment thick; as a result each apartment has cross-ventilation. In Senn and Mock's well-planned apartment in Basel (page 310), the all-glass end of the living rooms gives not only light and air, but an agreeable feeling of open spaciousness. In pleasant weather, the balcony beyond is used as part of the living room.

The economic advantages of the apartment house can logically be projected much further, and herald one of the great post-war achievements—low-cost housing.

TECTON and LUBETKIN: High-point Flats. Highgate, London. 1935

The tall building leaves land free for a large garden, swimming pool, tennis and squash courts. Each apartment has at least two good exposures, and is entered directly from the elevator; there are no corridors. Construction: monolithic reinforced concrete.

Rents for 3- and 4-room apartments run from about $600 to $1000 a year.

309

Otto SENN and Rudolf MOCK: Zosse Apartments. Basel, Switzerland. 1936

Four floors of apartments cantilevered out over a ground floor containing maids' rooms, laundry, etc. Sliding steel sash form continuous bands of glass. Top apartments have 2-story glass walled living-rooms and private roof gardens. All share common roof garden.

HOUSING

In domestic architecture, nothing today is more important than public housing. As the skyscraper is the typical American monument of the boom of the 20's, public housing may well be the true monument of the 40's. *The Government has already set aside $800,000,000 for housing.*

The problem is of course not purely architectural. Legal, financial, sociological aspects are of primary importance. These must be passed over in an exhibition concerned with architecture, particularly with design. Good architectural design is as essential to good housing as substantial construction. For the millions of citizens who will live in them, housing developments will become a formative part of their environment. An efficiently planned environment is essential for physical needs; an agreeably designed environment is essential for psychological well-being. A healthy, happy and vigorous population is a matter of vital concern to all for economic as well as humanitarian reasons.

In their pioneering, architects of private houses have explored three fields fruitful for low-rent housing as well. The first is the free open plan; space efficiently organized can accommodate more people and give each more space and more amenities than can traditional room planning. The second is the development of new and standard pre-fabricated parts; a housing architect draws increasingly upon mass-produced parts which were originally custom-made for richer individual clients. The third contribution is esthetic—intangible but none the less real and important.

The design of thousand foot housing façades may seem remote from that of the private house. The influence of the latter has not always been direct—the front of a good housing block does not, for instance, look like many houses joined together—but the *rational attitude* of the architect toward the evolution of his design is the same in both cases.

The Minimum Needs

Modern housing has had to focus relentlessly on the basic needs of the average family in order to provide decent habitation for those unable to afford it with their own resources. It has been necessary to modify sentimental conceptions of the "home" and banish any delusions of monumental or façade planning. In this concentration on essential requirements lies the chief difference between pre- and post-war housing. Good architecture has been made out of necessities alone. In successful housing developments handsome design and agreeable setting are considered necessities, not luxuries.

Site Planning

Sunlight, drainage and ventilation are primary concerns of the housing architect. Respecting the practical engineering requirements of street layout, grading, draining and the economies resulting from minimizing excavation, he must modify his ideal solution by adjusting it to specific site conditions. By relating the direction of sunlight to the layout of separate apartments, it has become possible to plan low-cost developments in which every living unit enjoys sun in every room every day. In America, under the leadership of the late Henry Wright, rigid European theories of uniformly

311

spaced buildings were modified to make use of attractive hillside sites hitherto rejected.

Landscaping

A parallel revolution has transformed the landscaping of housing developments and continues under the peculiar economic conditions surrounding American housing today. The ideas of symmetrical planning have been supplanted by arrangements of space as rational as those evolved for the planning of living quarters; the arbitrary division between formal and naturalistic gardening has given way to designs emphasizing usefulness. Open spaces have been transformed into play areas for children and pleasant gardens and recreational areas for their parents (page 325).

Standardization

More systematic thought has been spent on the design of the minimum-cost dwelling in the last twenty years than in the previous five thousand. Mass production of standardized doors and windows and equipment like bathtubs, cupboards and heaters has been the most effective factor in lowering costs. At the same time, standardized parts and equipment have benefited from the expert knowledge of architects and home economists and the standard of living has been raised even in the minimum-cost home.

The process of building large scale developments is very different from that of constructing single houses. Today's application of the principles of mass-production lies not only in the use of pre-fabricated elements but also in the intelligent planning of the entire building process as a huge and rapid manufacturing job to be executed on the site. The standardization of many individual parts is tending to reduce building operations to a sort of assembly-line production technique similar to that employed in our factories. In these developments America has again pioneered, in large part because in America we have had a greater opportunity to build on a large scale. The assembly of a skyscraper demonstrates American organizing talent; it is precisely from this kind of operation that the principles of economical construction of dwelling units have developed. These possibilities of large scale building operations, coupled with certain economic factors in land assembly and management, have made the large neighborhood housing project far more advantageous than the erection of isolated dwellings for an equivalent number of people. Complete with all its necessary community facilities, it is an undertaking of the first magnitude: nowhere is the happy union of intelligent design and scientific planning more rewarding.

European Housing

A generation's work in housing in Europe has stored up an accumulation of experience for which the American architect may well be thankful. Though conditions often differ the housing problem is so similar the world over that substantial gains in one country can soon be made to benefit another.

Germany and England saw the first important developments of European housing. Community housing was implicit in the English garden city movement proclaimed by Sir Ebenezer Howard (1902), and though only two garden cities have been built in England the idea has been of great significance. English housing densi-

312

ties and the space provisions of individual suites are today of a higher standard than those of almost any other European country. In many respects they are higher than our own.

In poverty-stricken Germany after the war a point of view known as "die neue Sachlichkeit" (the new objectivity) was elaborated into an almost antiseptic esthetic. It found expression in painting, music and films, but especially in architecture and above all in the minimum-cost dwelling. The Social Democratic government sponsored a housing movement of tremendous social and architectural significance. Despite inflation and other economic calamities 12,000,000 people, one-fifth of the whole nation, was re-housed. The Germans, as would be expected, rationally systematized housing techniques. They evolved the *Siedlung*, or complete housing community with stores, theatres and other community services. Often, as at Siemensstadt (page 320), they made of the necessities of minimal-cost dwellings fine simple designs, masterly in their honest multiplication of the few essential features. Row-planning (*Zeilenbau*) was developed with an insistence on proper orientation and through ventilation; this entailed units one apartment thick.

Germany was able in an impressive number of projects to demonstrate that efficient low-cost housing could become distinguished architecture.

Holland is particularly noteworthy for the efficient management of its large housing communities. Vienna under the socialist regime was girdled by huge apartment blocks undistinguished in design but notable for the method of their financing by real estate taxes and by the profits from city-owned public utilities. Sweden has outstripped other countries in cooperative housing; whole cooperative communities have been built (page 319). In France the unbuilt theoretical schemes of Le Corbusier have perhaps been more significant than any buildings actually constructed. The isolated skyscrapers at Drancy (page 323) are an experimental reinterpretation of his ideas. In Finland Aalto has built new projects superbly adapted to their fine sites, some with tall apartment buildings which may be of greater relevance to America than anything yet done abroad. In Russia the integration of housing with city-planning seems to have been pushed further than anywhere else, a development which may well be expected to affect our own planning.

LE CORBUSIER: Model for "La Ville Radieuse." 1922-5

American Housing

Before the impetus given it in 1933 by government building American housing was largely a theoretical exercise. Pleasant exceptions were to be seen at Sunnyside, Long Island, and Radburn, New Jersey, the last a valuable study in town planning because of its recognition of the essentially American problem of heavy motor traffic. In this early scheme the houses turned their backs on the widely separated streets and faced inward to large park-like greens in the center of each great super-block.

PWA

In 1933 the Public Works Administration inaugurated a centralized housing program; a Housing Division was organized to design and build. In the following five years 20,000 dwelling units were opened in more than fifty projects which, despite rents which were still too high, reached income groups whose interests were neglected in private building operations. But few of these projects are as important for the future of American housing as are many European projects. The architects generally employed were pitifully unfamiliar with the problems with which they were dealing and many developments were marred by shadowboxing with supposed public taste and the tragic heritage of bad speculative building in the United States.

Organized labor sponsored the first large project undertaken by the PWA, Carl Mackley Houses in Philadelphia

314

(1934). Unfortunately the quality of housing design seems to have retrogressed from this fine beginning—sober but not severe, reasonable and distinguished in its handling of familiar everyday materials. Even Westfield Acres (page 330), though largely the work of one of the same architects, has not been able to surpass the pleasant and quiet simplicity of its distinguished forerunner. Not large for a housing project, Carl Mackley Houses were developed within the inexorable frame of the Philadelphia street system. The buildings are well oriented for light and air; the window areas are large; and the planning of each family unit sound and advanced; there are attractive community facilities. As far as standards are concerned we might easily have done worse: as far as design is concerned we actually have done a great deal worse.

Williamsburg, largely through the efforts of Lescaze, enjoys perhaps the most skillfully worked out parallel orientation in America (page 324). The angle at which all the buildings are set is not determined by the Brooklyn streets surrounding them but by a nice calculation of the direction of summer and winter sunlight and wind. City officials wrecked the opportunity of completing a truly important work in harmonious design when they wantonly reared a commonplace school in the middle of the composition, parallel to the streets it does not flank and awkwardly at variance with the carefully oriented buildings around it. Trumbull Park (page 326) is probably the most uncompromising of all PWA projects in its site plan. Parallel row-housing has there been carried further than elsewhere, on a grand scale and with fine results.

In esthetic quality American housing at first lagged far behind contemporary European work. Faced with the problem of a thousand foot façade American designers have quailed, introducing unnecessary projections, varying the roof-line or inventing other unjustified irregularities.

PWA: Carl Mackley Houses, Juniata Park. Philadelphia. 1934-5. W. Pope Barney, Supervising Architect. Stonorov & Kastner, Designers

315

They have tried to transform the naturally simple and regular large scale housing block into artificial approximations of more familiar domestic building.

In Europe the most successful material for large scale housing has been reinforced concrete. Largely from habit American architects have chosen traditional brick, wishing to benefit by apparent economies in American building practice but forgetting that building practice is a result of large scale demand and that a large scale demand created by housing operations might easily affect building practice.

Whereas European houses have discarded the sloping roof (wasteful of space and uneconomical in most materials), American architects have clung to it, seemingly through a reluctance to break from the "cottage" school of design. This is why apartment block projects usually look more "modern" than projects with rows of self-consciously "homey" houses.

In the working out of their standard plans for the family unit PWA houses were closer to American speculative building than to advanced European housing— small parlors and large bedrooms, separate kitchens, etc. Windows were unforgivably small. Conservative design-habits account for the curiously compromised appearance of so many PWA housing projects. Behind these and other errors stood a stupid officialdom which refused to recognize the enormous progress already made elsewhere.

Resettlement Administration

Concurrently with the PWA housing program, the Resettlement Administration was building a series of suburban garden city developments called "greenbelt"

towns from the park-like zone surrounding them. In Greendale (page 329) the Radburn ideas of site planning have been extended until a wholly American type of suburban planning has been evolved, perhaps the most interesting arrangement in all Resettlement projects. In Greenbelt (page 328) on a conscientiously adjusted community plan stand gaily colored row houses and well designed three-story apartment groups.

USHA

The housing activities of the Government were consolidated and made permanent when the United States Housing Authority was created late in 1937. A wholly new foundation for American housing was laid, and a decentralized program begun. Whereas the Resettlement Administration and the PWA employed their own architects and designed and built their own housing developments, the USHA restricts its efforts to financing, standard-setting and education. All housing design, building and management are entrusted to local authorities. These new organizations are, like park commissions or boards of education, semi-independent departments of the city administration. They choose sites, hire architects, borrow money from the USHA, and, by issuing their own bonds, build housing projects and operate them under fixed regulations guaranteeing low rentals. The USHA can insist on certain standards in planning and design.

In nearly 200 communities throughout the country local housing authorities have already been created and are inaugurating housing projects of their own. The $800,000,000 which Congress has authorized the USHA to lend has already been allocated on the basis of provisional plans

316

and additional funds are being authorized by Congress.

What types of housing will these new authorities build? What standards will determine their design? How will they compare with previous work in this country and with work abroad? The situation resulting from the new legislation is still changing too much, and the number of projects for which final designs have been drawn is still too small to permit any final judgment. From the first group it is gratifyingly clear, however, that we may expect projects surpassing those of the PWA both in efficiency and quality of design. In the handling of free space in the larger projects traditional inhibitions are disappearing; American landscape practice seems to have outstripped European. And in the planning of the suites for single families spaciousness is being gained through ingenious adaptations of the open plan.

Local housing authorities and their architects are becoming more venturesome in the use of new materials and more inventive in experimenting with new building methods, particularly in California, Texas and other parts of the country where architecture in general has been progressive. As in Europe, leaders in housing design are architects distinguished also in other fields.

The design of housing projects is a stimulating task. "Freed from the degrading job of being a handy man of the realtor working only for the great game of land exploitation, he (the architect) found a way to devote all his talents exclusively to the practical, technical and architectural problems of housing. Now, for the first time, it became his task to develop, in accordance with actual and clearly defined needs, and with all the aid of technical science, a new type of small dwelling."[1]

Few things are as vital to the future of our country and of every city in it as the proper solution of the housing problem. And good design is a vital part of that problem. The future of public housing rests with the architects, with the local authorities who choose them and set the problem and with the public which supports the movement and will live in the houses. Let us hope that we can take full advantage of this magnificent opportunity to improve our country not only with unprecedented social benefits but also a living and handsome architecture.

FREDERICK GUTHEIM and
JOHN MCANDREW

[1] W. C. Behrendt, *Modern Building, Its Nature, Problems, and Forms*, New York, Harcourt, Brace and Co., 1937.

ARTARIA & SCHMIDT, M. E. HÄ-FELI, HUBACHER & STEIGER, MOSER & ROTH: Neubühl. Zürich-Wollishofen, Switzerland. 1929-31

A loop of streets off the main road leads to the colony of houses and their accessory shops, kindergarten, garages and recreation building. Because of the slight hill, and because the rows of houses are short and widely spaced, every living-room opens out to the south-east with a fine view of the Lake of Zürich. (photo Swissair)

318

Architects' Office of the KF, Eskil SUNDAHL, chief architect: Kvarn-holmen. Sweden. 1927-35

On this island in Stockholm Harbor the Whole-sale Cooperative Society (KF) maintains fac-tories for macaroni and "crisp-bread" and, on the wooded slope nearest the mainland, dwell-ings for the factory employees. Conveniently near are the recreation building and general store.

←

Walter GROPIUS: Siemensstadt Siedlung. Berlin. 1929

A distinguished design based necessarily on the most severe logic and economy. Minimum-cost apartment blocks for the lowest-income group of the community.

Arne JACOBSEN: Bellavista Flats. Bellevue, Denmark. 1934-35

Sixty-eight apartments built as a private enterprise at a beach resort in the royal forest 15 minutes from Copenhagen. The staggered plan gives excellent light and privacy to each apartment. A smooth green lawn, uninterrupted by planting, meets in a clean line the white buildings unencumbered by unnecessary detail.

GATEPAC: Workmen's Dwellings.
Barcelona. 1935

More than half of this project of the Barcelona Workmen's Housing Committee had been completed and occupied before the outbreak of the war.

The scheme is well adapted to the Mediterranean climate, for the wings are very widely spaced, and each of the 4-room duplex apartments has sizeable balconies front and back. The building is raised on columns; the whole site is left open for recreation. There are club rooms, swimming pool, library, nursery school and children's gardens.

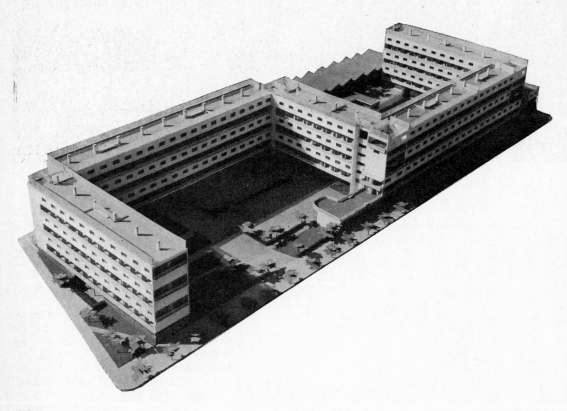

BEAUDOUIN and LODS: Cité de la Muette. Drancy (near Paris). 1934

If finished, this will be a complete community with its own schools, church, athletic fields, recreation building, shops, and even common central heating. Financed by the State.

The well-spaced skyscrapers assure their tenants light, air and privacy; their location at the north of the entire group prevents their shadows from falling on occupied spaces. Despite structural and mechanical flaws, this scheme shows an important type of housing solution unrealized elsewhere.

PWA: Williamsburg Houses. Brooklyn, N. Y. 1937. R. H. Shreve, Chief Architect. Bly, Del Gaudio, Holden, Lescaze, Gardstein, Trapani, Gurney, Walker, Ingle, Associates

An oasis of open space and comfortable orderly buildings in the middle of a blighted slum area. Only 30% of the land is built on.

The regular gridiron of the city street-system has been modified to triple-size super-blocks. This reduces the dangerous through-streets and permits a more advantageous arrangement of the buildings. (photo Fairchild)

1622 families. Average rent for 1 room for 1 month: $7.12.

→

PWA: Cedar Central Apartments. Cleveland. 1937. Walter R. McCornack, Architect

Three-story apartment blocks shelter the park-like lawn in the center from wind and too much summer sun; they also shut away the noise and ugly sight of surrounding slums. (photo PWA)

650 families. Average rent 1 room 1 month: $5.71.

324

PWA: Trumbull Park Homes. Chicago. 1937. John A. Holabird, Chief Architect, Armstrong, Jensen, Maher, Grunsfeld, Chatten, Merrill, Walcott, Huszagh, Hodgdon, Associates

A large scheme with unusual regularity in the placing of long rows of buildings and uniformity in their design. In its large-scale simplicity it is comparable to good German work before 1932. (photo USHA-Sekaer)

462 families. Rent 1 room for 1 month: $5.43.

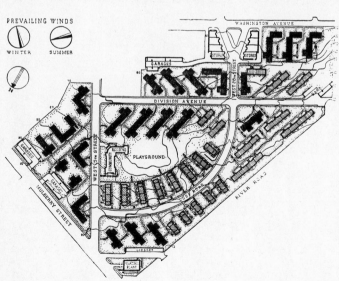

PREVAILING WINDS

WINTER   SUMMER

PWA: Lakeview Terrace. Cleveland. 1937. J. L. Weinberg, Chief Architect

Ingenious exploitation of a dramatic site overlooking Lake Erie, yet close to the heart of the **city.** (photo USHA-Sekaer)

▬▬ 3-story apartments

▨▨ 2-story row-houses

||||||| 2- & 3-story, arranged in steps on the hillside

620 families. Rent 1 room for 1 month: $5.84.

327

FSA: Greenbelt. Berwyn, Maryland. 1937. Hale Walker, Town Planner. Ellington & Wadsworth, Architects

Community plan developed directly from this specific site.

In the hollow are the community buildings, circled above by roads which follow the contour of the slopes. Set back from the roads, usually at right angles to them are apartments and row-houses connected by foot-paths.

885 families. Average rent 1 room for 1 month: $5.90.

FSA: Greendale (near Milwaukee), Wisconsin. 1938. Crane & Peets, Town Planners. Bentley & Thomas, Architects

A whole town of separate and semi-detached houses, with school, shopping center and recreational facilities. New and indigenous design elements, with economical combination of new and indigenous ways of building (cinder-block houses with ordinary wood-framed gable roofs).

572 families. Average rent 1 room for 1 month: $5.91.

←

USHA: Westfield Acres. Camden, N. J. 1938. Joseph N. Hettel, Chief Architect. MacNelly, Radey, Gill, Stonorov, Moffett, Hall, Jefferis, Neutze, Associates

Minimum cost buildings need not be barren in design.

Skillful composition making use of only the absolute necessities, windows, buff brick walls and chimneys, concrete balconies, etc. (photo Lincoln)

Available to all tenants: Social hall, 10 centralized laundries, garages.

514 families. Average rent 1 room for 1 month: $4.89.

PWA: Dixie Homes (for Negroes). Memphis, Tenn. 1937. G. Frazier Smith and Associates, Architects

PWA: Central Office. La Granja. Puerto Rico. 1937

PWA: Central Office. Mirapalmeras. Puerto Rico. 1937

PWA: Central Office. H. H. Berg Homes. St. Thomas, Virgin Islands. 1937

Projects especially designed for hot climates.

INDUSTRIAL
DESIGN

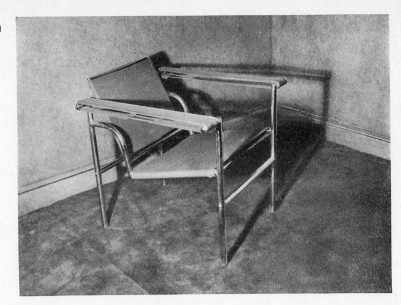

LE CORBUSIER

Steel chair with adjustable back.
1929

Ludwig MIËS VAN DER ROHE

First steel chair with spring legs,
1927

Marcel BREUER

Plywood reclining chair, 1932-5

Alvar AALTO

Chair with plywood seat, 1930

Buckminster FULLER

"One-piece" bathroom, 1926-38. A very compact bathroom unit hamper in sheet metal (like an automobile body). Prefabricated in mass production, it would be much less expensive than the usual bathroom. It is also easier to keep clean since dust adheres to the special metal surface less even than to porcelain.

334

A REVIEW OF FILM HISTORY IN A CYCLE OF 70 FILMS

In the motion picture, youngest and most popular of the arts, a new vehicle of expression was discovered. Its early history is strikingly unlike that of the other arts, but the stages through which it is developing and the potentialities which lie before it offer a field of wide interest. Happily, it is no longer necessary to rely entirely on written material and on memory for a knowledge of those phases through which the motion picture has evolved during the forty-four years of its existence. Gradually, the films which themselves wrote that history are being recovered and made available for re-examination and assessment. This work of restoring vanished motion pictures to view is the primary, though by no means the only, undertaking of the Film Library of the Museum of Modern Art. From its archives of films acquired for preservation, programs of motion pictures illustrating various phases in the history of this vital medium are gradually being made accessible to students in colleges and museums throughout the country. Ultimately the sum of these programs will provide material for a complete analysis of the early development of a new art: the films already on hand make possible a survey of the main body of film-making from 1895 onwards.

Normally the Film Library's programs are shown only to members of educational or cultural institutions and groups, but not to the general public: this is one of the conditions on which they have been placed in the custody of the Museum. Throughout the present summer, however, permission has been obtained to exhibit films to the visitors to the Museum's new building. A cycle of thirty programs of motion pictures will therefore be shown, day by day, in the Museum auditorium from May to October and will be open to non-members.[1] The entire cycle, comprising some seventy films, illustrates major steps in the development of the new medium from 1895, through the era of silent films and the rise and development of talking pictures. It includes such classics as *The Birth of a Nation**, *The Cabinet of Dr. Caligari**, *Little Caesar** and the first Mickey Mouse.

The cycle though extensive does not provide an entire outline of the film's history: the Film Library is a pioneer in this field and the recovery and preservation of motion pictures is not merely a lengthy and a costly undertaking but a difficult one, so hedged about is the use of film with human, technical and legal obstacles. There are some obvious omissions, such as the lack of Russian films. This will be remedied when the Film Library next year adds to its circulating programs the group of pictures from pre-revolutionary Russia and the U.S.S.R. which it has acquired. Then the later films of René Clair, though destined eventually for the Library's collection, are still in general distribution and are therefore not available through these channels. A number of Chaplin's early films, already in

[1] In the following pages an asterisk following the title of a film indicates that the film is included in these programs.

the archives, are being held back against the day when Chaplin sees his way to contribute such highly desirable examples of his later work as *Shoulder Arms, The Pilgrim* or *The Gold Rush.* The progressive spectacle of his development, from his early days with Mack Sennett to the years of his maturity, should then be compensation enough for the absence here of a representation of this artist's work.

1895: Lumière's **Lunch Hour at the Factory**

The first movies

With the earliest films shown here, it is possible to turn back in imagination to the end of the last century and see afresh the screen fare which at first so obscurely and so humbly but with increasing persuasiveness caught the attention and finally won the affection of audiences all over the world. A startling novelty at the time, the first little fifty-foot "living pictures" were looked at with amazement and without criticism. They were run at the end of vaudeville shows, or shown in fairgrounds and no one envisaged their future. It is not difficult to perceive, however, that right from the beginning, films were of two distinct kinds. Lumière's *Lunch-Hour at the Factory** and *Arrival of a Train**, for instance, are simple records of events or scenes in real life, whereas in *The Execution of Mary Queen of Scots** and *Wash Day Troubles** the subject was specially staged or improvised for the camera. It is an important distinction which has persisted to this day: we have newsreels, travelogues and documentary pictures as well as studio-manufactured movies. But at first it was the films of fact which seem most to have impressed and pleased spectators—they marveled to see motion picture photography of regiments on the march, street traffic and wild animals, as faraway places and familiar scenes alike were brought to life so vividly on the screen.

Gradually the films of enacted scenes began to predominate and it was not long until longer subjects developed and, eventually, a definite plot, as in Méliès, *A Trip to the Moon.** As might have been expected, the direction along which the film traveled was at first uncertain: blind alleys were explored and there were many false starts and hesitations. After 1908 an effort was made in France to raise the status of the new medium by persuading well known stage personalities to appear on the screen in photographed versions of familiar plays. This resulted in a succession of films culminating in the famous *Queen Elizabeth** of Sarah Bernhardt.

Queen Elizabeth founded the fortunes of one large American film company and converted large numbers of people to the

1912: **Queen Elizabeth,** with Sarah Bernhardt.

hitherto despised screen, but it was fundamentally an imitation of the theatre and hardly film at all. Something much more important was being attempted in far simpler pictures—farcical affairs with funny characters capering around such as we see in *The Runaway Horse**, or blood-and-thunder melodramas which were enjoyed rather than admired, such as the rightly famous *Great Train Robbery** of Edwin S. Porter. Here, in striking contrast both to Méliès' *Trip to the Moon* and Mercanton's much later *Queen Elizabeth*, we see a bold attempt to tell a story full of action in an original manner and with distinctly cinematic freedom. The limitations of space and time which bind the theatre and those films which copy the theatrical style are bravely thrown away: the action whisks from point to point as the director

chooses. Porter had definitely found a technique proper to the screen and like nothing else in the world. From that day until the present time the cinema has developed Porter's discoveries, though at times abandoning them so that we have had many films which were in effect plays. Cinema has never quite known whether it is more at home with play-acting or with its own affairs. This is as true today as it was thirty years ago when the Italians produced a series of elaborate spectacles, usually in classical settings and in a curiously operatic style—gesticulation, wigs, togas, temples, seething mobs and captions to tell the story. Yet this whole group of pictures, (*Quo Vadis* and *Cabiria* are best remembered) played a useful part in encouraging film-makers boldly to tackle imposing subjects and in enticing

337

1903: Edwin S. Porter's **The Great Train Robbery.**

new audiences into the cinemas. Such films were felt to be, though rather confusedly, somehow improving and even educational.

Early masters of the American film

From 1908 to 1916 the American film industry gradually established itself and the American film, following the example set by the French and Italian films of the period, increased in length from one reel —in 1903 considered very long—to eight or more. As it grew in size it acquired a new vitality, a new expressiveness and a wider technical range, discovering at the same time the sort of subject-matter best suited to it. During these years Thomas H. Ince, Mack Sennett and D. W. Griffith came into prominence.

The name of Ince became associated chiefly with the Western melodramas in which William S. Hart and his pony typified the artless but heroic morality of a vanished and perhaps imaginary frontier. Cowboys and Indians had appeared on the screen at a very early date but, as *The Fugitive** shows, Ince understood how to inject emotions as well as action into Western films and by dextrous cutting to add suspense and meaning to his simple plots. If what he had to say was not profound, he had a curious eloquence.

Mack Sennett, in different vein, set out to imitate early French farces like *The Runaway Horse* but stamped the formula with that fantastic nature which has been celebrated in Gene Fowler's book, *Father Goose.* The unreasonable and often irresistibly funny series of chases, tum-

338

bles, humiliations which provided his subject-matter seem, in retrospect, best characterized by the absurd Keystone cops and dainty bathing belles who appeared in so many Sennett pictures. The slap-stick film created a noble band of grotesque figures—buffoons of lugubrious appearance, enraged matrons, desperate crooks armed with harmless bombs—who captured the world's fancy. Films were still not very respectable in those days but it was impossible to keep children out of them and, inevitably, adults fol-lowed. The Keystone comedies were mag-nificently vulgar and crammed with comic inventions: often they displayed satiric humor, for they respected nothing. In 1913 the strange group that produced them was joined by a newcomer, Charles Chaplin, who graduating later from this excellent school added to what he had learnt there his own exquisite sense of comic timing, a profound observation of life and a note of tragic resignation. Two other comedians, Harold Lloyd and Buster Keaton, also stemmed from the same source—Lloyd, as in *The Freshman**, typifying the simple fellow who inno-cently courts danger but never recognizes it, and Keaton, as in *The Navigator**, patiently applying his own crazy logic to a world which he clearly regards as mad.

The work of the third of the three great "early masters" of the American film, D. W. Griffith, is so well represented in the present programs that it speaks for itself. During his initial period Griffith was at his best in handling intimate situa-tions, as in *The New York Hat**, where the relatively brief close-up, medium and long shots are already joined together in such manner as to convey more than they actually depict. There is less action, cer-tainly, than in Sennett's and Ince's films but there is also more meaning, more hu-manity and a much greater wealth of suggestion. Griffith was discovering how to make the images on the screen com-municate thoughts as well as feelings, and he was well-served by the able camera-man, G. W. Bitzer, who worked with him for many years, and by the company of very young players he drew to himself. Mary Pickford's acting in this quaint little piece is already accomplished and subtly expressive: it is screen-acting and not anything else.

*The Birth of a Nation** makes apparent how important was Griffith's contribution. Here spectacle alternates with intimate drama and intensifies it. Time has made certain of its elements a little laughable but the complex construction of the film's best sequences cannot fail, even today, to command respect: it is with amazement that one observes alike the photography and the emotional force of the battle scenes. The ugly passions and prejudices inherent in the story on which the film was based, and to which unfortunately *The Birth of a Nation* owes part of its success, must not be attributed to Griffith. He did not retell that story of civil war and subsequent evils with any base in-tent and was, indeed, amazed at the criti-cism which the film met. He replied to it with his astonishing *Intolerance** where, in an attempt to hunt down prejudice through the ages, he narrated four stories at once and developed his staccato style into a perfect torrent of movement which is exhausting though magnificent. By the time he made *Broken Blossoms**, his man-ner seems less instinctive and free and even a trifle arty, but this—like his greater films—exerted a wide influence and, at the time, moved audiences profoundly.

339

Way Down East*, despite its plot, once more demonstrated his brilliant faculty for creating suspense and even hysteria by his calculated and flexible technique.

The golden 'twenties

As film-making became more lucrative and the American film more and more dominant, a new set of circumstances arose. This country continued to supply the world with the bulk of its screen-fare, designed to appeal to the largest possible number of people by providing them with day-dreams made concrete and second-hand adventures. This was the era of vamps, sheiks, boudoirs, "It"-girls and white haired mothers. During it hundreds of forgotten films mirrored and influenced a generation that took for granted prohibition and faith in the full dinner-pail. Technical advances appeared more often than new kinds of films, and the actors and actresses on the screen came to seem more important than the characters they portrayed or the stories they appeared in. Few of the men who made films had the liberty or the courage to attempt experiments, so that the desperately realistic *Greed** of von Stroheim, for instance, stands out in almost disproportionate relief amid the flood of glamorous romances and glittering spectacles produced during the early 'twenties. Von Stroheim was attempting to force the screen to mirror life, but at its darkest. Now and then other men, too, broke with studio tradition, as when Robert Flaherty gave us first *Nanook* and then *Moana of the South Seas** and James Cruze sought to recapture the authentic appearance and spirit of frontier days in *The Covered Wagon**. Other elements in it may seem obvious, but Rex Ingram's *Four Horse-*

men of the Apocalypse*, too, was a bold experiment in 1921—the war as a subject had been taboo for three years and the story itself is a queer mixture of sophistication and of moralizing, both usually regarded as difficult subjects. Though the film is best remembered because it brought Rudolph Valentino into prominence, it remains a curious reflection of popular feeling at the time and provides an interesting contrast with King Vidor's later war-film, *The Big Parade**.

Transatlantic activity

During the 'twenties, some important discoveries and experiments were being undertaken in Europe. Nationalistic feeling dictated fresh efforts at competition with the all-conquering American product and films, as a whole, were taken more seriously than in this country. In Sweden, somewhat earlier, a new school of cinematography had been founded by the two directors Victor Seastrom and Mauritz Stiller, both of whom were undoubtedly influenced by American cowboy films and by Griffith but whose pictures invariably dealt with Scandinavian tradition, landscape and character. In their own sober and impressive way they discovered how to depict human life in a freshly rich and truthful fashion, and by various devices to imply or stress motive and mood. Both of these directors ultimately came to work in America. Seastrom made several films in Hollywood which earned admiration if not the widest success—*The Tower of Lies*, with Norma Shearer and Lon Chaney, deserves to be remembered as well as *The Wind**—and then returned to Sweden. Though Stiller died in 1928, the romantic spirit his films evoked still lingers in the fragment of *Hotel Imperial**

340

shown here, and in the earlier and greater picture, *The Story of Gösta Berling**, in which Greta Garbo played her first important role.

Meanwhile the film in Germany had begun to develop rapidly and here the influence of the theatre was once more felt. This time, however, it was the influence of the new, experimental theatre and it brought with it certain unfamiliar elements—a deliberation of pace, a preoccupation with lighting effects and with décor, and a marked interest in the darker aspects of character and of psychology. *The Cabinet of Dr. Caligari** and *The Last Laugh**, with Emil Jannings, were widely discussed and they, too, drew new audiences to the cinema. But the former, a horror story in an Expressionist setting, had little influence save on theoreticians whereas the latter (together with other films in the same style) caused a whole new method of set-construction, of lighting and of camerawork to be adopted in Hollywood and elsewhere. Now German directors and technicians were imported wholesale into the American studios and, wherever it was possible to substitute a movement of the camera for a simple cut, then cameras were moved—often with little justification. How far this tendency was carried may best be judged in *Sunrise**, made by the director of *The Last Laugh* but produced in Hollywood at tremendous expense in sets the size of small villages. The influence of German films can be detected in less marked manner in Douglas Fairbanks' *Thief of Bagdad* and *Robin Hood**, in the construction and lighting of the sets and, for that matter, in the new trend towards costume pieces.

Advance-guard films in France

The French film had not recovered the vitality of its first years but, after the war, there were more free experiments carried on in France than elsewhere. The critical French spirit had long since begun to examine the motion picture with intelligence as well as with enjoyment. It ceased, very early in France, to seem remarkable that cultivated persons should admit to a love of the cinema. A new generation which admired Griffith and Sennett, and felt that to make good movies was as praiseworthy as to paint good pictures or write good plays, now turned back for inspiration to the earliest days of the cinema and sought to recapture the spontaneity and simplicity of the primitives. This attitude is evident in René Clair's first picture, *The Crazy Ray**, which recalls the trick-films that pioneers like Méliès and Zecca had made years before. It also recaptures something of the purely photographic (as opposed to picturesque) quality of Lumière's first offerings and uses natural settings as unaffectedly as *Fantomas**, the serial which had provided delicious shudders for the pre-war generation. His second picture, *Entr'acte** together with the painter Fernand Léger's stimulating *Ballet Mécanique**, records better than verbal description could the channels which the French advance-guard was so busily exploring. Both pictures have aged extraordinarily little in the intervening years. It is to be remarked that both of them say what they have to say without the use of subtitles, that the same is true of *The Last Laugh*, and that the two French films were made to be accompanied by special music regarded as an integral part of their structure.

341

From Subtitles to Sound

Without re-examining the silent films (whose disappearance one is sometimes tempted to regret), it is impossible to realize how sorely overburdened they often were with written matter. Too often the story was told in subtitles interspersed with illustrative matter. There were films in which one-third of the total footage consisted of subtitles. We are apt to forget, too, the role that music had come to play in the theatres and that movie orchestras were amply provided with machines for making various sounds—thunder, hoof-beats, rifle-shots, bird-calls and the like. Perhaps the future should have been evident: but no one, not even the members of the film industry, quite realized what had happened when in 1926-7 talking films made a modest appearance. They were not exactly an innovation, for talking films of sorts had been introduced before, though not with success. This time the problem of amplifying mechanically-reproduced sound, as well as recording and reproducing it, had finally been solved: yet when in 1926 a few Vitaphone shorts appeared very few people indeed realized that a revolution was at hand. Even when the Movietone newsreel came along it was accepted as an interesting novelty in a particular field and although, very shortly after this, in the fateful *Jazz Singer** Al Jolson spoke a few words and sang a couple of songs, it was still difficult to foresee what was imminent. That was in 1927. By 1930 virtually nothing but talking films were being made in America and some of that year's best ones were coming from abroad.

A review of most of the early talking films provides sad disillusionment. When they appeared originally their very novelty made a strong appeal, but today they seem crude. To begin with, one finds with astonishment how coarse and disagreeable the actual quality of early sound was. Moreover, since the method of sound pick-up was limited, the actors had to stand still near the microphone and scenes could only be cut when the talking was over. This necessarily sacrificed that freedom of movement which the camera had won for itself, and the first talkies were woefully dull to the eye. The ear was not better served, since early attempts at dialogue were pompous and clumsy. Fortunately a living art can easily assimilate new elements, and the film emerged from the doldrums with surprising speed. Thanks to the technicians—and the film technicians are often far in advance of what is demanded of them—the camera soon regained its freedom, while improved methods of sound-recording have since restored complete flexibility to the medium. There is less dialogue and it is more natural.

The transition period is vividly recalled by *The Love Parade**, *Anna Christie** and *Cavalcade**. Fundamentally little more than canned plays, they nevertheless struggle to be something else: *The Love Parade* has absurd moments (as when the heroine in bed bursts into song upon an obvious cue) but the opening scene is pure visual naughtiness, equal to Lubitsch's best in the silent days, and he combined sight with sound in a manner quite novel by moving his camera away from Chevalier as he bids his musical farewell to Paris. *Anna Christie* drags abominably while the characters respectfully pronounce Mr. O'Neill's lines, but audiences were thrilled in 1930 to hear Miss Garbo speak for the first time. The bright dialogue and heavy sentimentality

342

of Mr. Coward's play are emphasized in the screen version of *Cavalcade* but this, too, had progressed a long way from *The Jazz Singer* and *The Lights of New York*.

While the human characters on the screen were struggling with the difficulties imposed by the new device for recording speech and sound, Mickey Mouse made his bow to the world. Walt Disney, who had been quietly making animated cartoons since 1920, met with considerable difficulty in getting Mickey shown to the public but, once seen and heard, his triumph was assured. For one thing the mouse moved wherever his creator wished and, while he did not say much, his remarks were to the point. Mickey Mouse was more than a delicious and popular creation: he pointed the way to fresh efforts toward combining visible with audible content which have by no means yet been exhausted.

Realism and document

How far the talking film could progress, even in those first years, is shown by *All Quiet on the Western Front**, a remarkable and even brilliant piece nearly as effective today as it was nine years ago. In many ways closer to *The Birth of a Nation* than to most of its contemporaries, it utilized the new technical devices instead of being overwhelmed by them and suggests the sweep, the momentum and sincerity of the best of the silent films. Possibly because of *All Quiet's* painful subject and uncompromising manner film-goers seem to recall *Little Caesar**, made in the same year, even more vividly. It has often been pointed out what excellent service the gangster pictures, generally, performed for the screen. They had come into prominence at the end of the silent era but, under the new regime, they provided unusually effective material. The speech of gunmen may not be elegant but it is brief and graphic, and the tapping of machine-guns, squealing of brakes, groans and curses provided a lively accompaniment. Perhaps more important still, the gangster films dealt with real characters and real situations and the motion picture is sometimes happiest when it reflects life rather than dreams. Technically, *Little Caesar* is still crude, but it *moves*. Undeniably the gangster films were brutal and perhaps brutalizing: there is a case to be made out for the repressive measures directed against them, though possibly these might rather have been directed against the social conditions that created gangsters.

The cinema itself proceeded to study those conditions, notably in that remarkable film, *I Am a Fugitive from a Chain Gang,** with which the present series of programs closes. This film might well serve as a reminder that no amount of criticism need prevent the motion picture from bravely, if spasmodically, holding a mirror up to life, from giving rein to the missionary propensity it has continued to evince for over forty years while preserving its love of violent action, simple characters, strong situations and popular topics. Although the cinema may seem most often impelled toward pomposity, pseudo-romance and artificiality, yet the motion picture camera somehow does not lend itself easily to false values but prefers simple things and, even, the truth.

A review of past cinema-fare indicates how important a role the newsreel and other films of fact have always played. Throughout the first decade they provided the major portion of screen fare and if, later, newsreels and topical budgets featured trivial occurrences rather than news they have nevertheless recorded many major events in recent history in a manner previously unknown. A compilation of old newsreels is informative as no book could be. It was the Movietone newsreel which first introduced the talking pictures and first recorded natural speech. More recently, the March of Time has discovered a fresh approach to pictorial news, lending it that strongly controversial flavor which has been reflected, too, in the present use of documentary films to map, analyze or propagandize world and national problems and opinions.

Nothing is wholly new—not even color-film—and nothing has yet been exhausted in all the wide repertory which the motion picture has so energetically essayed. Despite the concrete rewards it offers its executants and exploiters, the film has endured and triumphed through its creative exuberance, not through its commercialism. From *The Great Train Robbery* to *Stagecoach* and *La Grande Illusion*, from Méliès to Disney, it has developed its technique and enriched its powers of expression, drawing greedily upon the traditional arts as well as upon life for its inspiration: but, in every country, the truly significant films which have marked the stages of its progress stand independent and unique, fit for comparison with the fiction, the painting or the drama of like date but utterly unlike them.

It would be foolish to minimize the immense contributions which America has made to the film's forward march: but in attempting to discern through many years and miles of celluloid what has been done in film that was best worth doing it becomes increasingly evident that advance has resulted always from the freest kind of international exchange and that many countries as well as many men have combined to confer upon the motion picture its peculiar importance and value in contemporary life.

IRIS BARRY

A Cycle of Seventy Films

1. THE DEVELOPMENT OF NARRATIVE
   - 1895 **The Execution of Mary Queen of Scots**
   - 1896 **Wash Day Troubles**
   - 1902 **A Trip to the Moon,** by Georges Méliès
   - 1903 **The Great Train Robbery,** by Edwin S. Porter (Edison)
   - 1910 **Faust,** a *Film d'Art*
   - 1912 **Queen Elizabeth,** with Sarah Bernhardt (Paramount)

2. THE RISE OF THE AMERICAN FILM
   - 1912 **The New York Hat,** directed by D. W. Griffith, with Mary Pickford and Lionel Barrymore (Miss Pickford)
   - 1914 **The Fugitive,** directed by Thomas H. Ince, with William S. Hart
   - 1914 **A Fool There Was,** with Theda Bara (Twentieth Century-Fox)
   - 1917 **The Clever Dummy,** a Mack Sennett comedy

3. THE BASIS OF MODERN TECHNIQUE
   - 1915 **The Birth of a Nation,** directed by D. W. Griffith, with H. B. Walthall, Lillian Gish, Mae Marsh (Epoch)

4. THE SOCIOLOGICAL FILM (I)
   - 1916 **Intolerance,** directed by D. W. Griffith, with Robert Harron, Mae Marsh, Miriam Cooper, Constance Talmadge (D. W. Griffith)

5. THE INTIMATE PHOTOPLAY
   - 1919 **Broken Blossoms,** directed by D. W. Griffith, with Lillian Gish, Richard Barthelmess and Donald Crisp (D. W. Griffith)

6. STAGE INTO SCREEN (I)
   - 1920 **Way Down East,** directed by D. W. Griffith, with Lillian Gish and Richard Barthelmess (Twentieth Century-Fox)

7. THE GERMAN FILM (I) Legend and Fantasy
   - 1896 Primitive German films by the pioneer Skladanowsky (Reichsfilmarchiv)
   - 1909 **Don Juan's Wedding,** with Giampietro (Reichsfilmarchiv)
   - c.1912 **Misunderstood,** with Henny Potren (Reichsfilmarchiv)
   - 1919 **The Cabinet of Dr. Caligari,** directed by Robert Wiene, with Werner Krauss and Conrad Veidt (Ufa)
   - 1920 **The Golem,** directed and interpreted by Paul Wegener—one sequence only (Ufa)

8. WAR IN RETROSPECT (I)
   1921 **The Four Horsemen of the Apocalypse,** directed by Rex Ingram, with Rudolph Valentino and Alice Terry (Loew's)

9. THE WESTERN FILM
   1903 **The Great Train Robbery,** directed by Edwin S. Porter (Edison)
   1915 **The Last Card,** directed by Thomas H. Ince, with William S. Hart
   1923 **The Covered Wagon,** directed by James Cruze (Paramount)

10. FAIRBANKS AND THE COSTUME PIECE
    1922 **Robin Hood,** directed by Allan Dwan, with Douglas Fairbanks (Fairbanks-United Artists)

11. THE SWEDISH FILM—Seastrom & Stiller
    1917 **The Outlaw and His Wife,** directed by Victor Seastrom—one sequence only (Svensk Filmindustri)
    1923-4 **The Story of Gösta Berling,** directed by Mauritz Stiller, with Lars Hanson and Greta Garbo (Svensk Filmindustri)

12. THE FRENCH FILM (I) From Lumière to René Clair
    1895 Films by Louis Lumière (Louis Lumière)
    1907 **The Runaway Horse**
    1913 **Fantômas,** directed by Louis Feuillade (Gaumont)
    1923 **The Crazy Ray** (Paris Qui Dort), directed by René Clair (J. S. Fairfax-Jones)

13. THE GERMAN FILM (II) The Moving Camera
    1921 **Hamlet,** directed by Svend Gade, with Asta Neilsen—one sequence only (Mrs. Philip Manson)
    1924 **The Last Laugh,** directed by F. W. Murnau, with Emil Jannings (Ufa)

14. VON STROHEIM THE REALIST
    1924 **Greed,** directed by Erich von Stroheim (Charles Norris—Loew's)

15. COMEDIES (I)
    1906 **Dream of a Rarebit Fiend,** by Edwin S. Porter (Edison)
    1920 **High and Dizzy,** directed by Hal Roach, with Harold Lloyd (Harold Lloyd)
    1924 **The Navigator,** directed by Donald Crisp and Buster Keaton, with Buster Keaton (Keaton—Loew's)

16. WAR IN RETROSPECT (II)
    1925 **The Big Parade,** directed by King Vidor (Loew's)

346

17. THE FRENCH FILM (II) The Advance-Guard
    1923 **The Smiling Madame Beudet,** directed by Germaine Dulac (Mme. Dulac)
    1924 **Entr'acte,** directed by René Clair (Fernand Léger)
    1925 **Ménilmontant,** directed by Dmitri Kirsanov (D. Kirsanov)
    1924 **Ballet Mécanique,** produced and directed by Fernand Léger (Fernand Léger)

18. ANCESTORS OF DOCUMENTARY
    1926 **Moana of the South Seas,** directed by Robert Flaherty (Harvard University Film Foundation)
    1927 **Berlin, The Symphony of a Big City,** directed by Walter Ruttmann (Reichsfilmarchiv)

19. THE GERMAN FILM (III) The New Realism
    1927 **The Love of Jeanne Ney,** directed by G. W. Pabst (Ufa)

20. COMEDIES (II)
    1908 **The Doctor's Secret,** by Georges Méliès
    1916 **His Bitter Pill,** a Mack Sennett satire
    1925 **The Freshman,** with Harold Lloyd (Harold Lloyd)
    1928 **The Sex Life of the Polyp,** with Robert Benchley (Twentieth Century-Fox)
    1929 **The Skeleton Dance,** by Walt Disney (Walt Disney)

21. THE SWEDISH-AMERICAN FILM
    1926-7 **Hotel Imperial,** directed by Mauritz Stiller, with Pola Negri—one sequence only (Paramount)
    1928 **The Wind,** directed by Victor Seastrom, with Lillian Gish and Lars Hanson (Loew's)

22. THE GERMAN-AMERICAN FILM
    1928 **Hands,** directed by Stella Simon (Mrs. Simon)
    1927 **Sunrise,** directed by F. W. Murnau, with George O'Brien and Janet Gaynor (Twentieth Century-Fox)

23. THE GANGSTER FILM (I)
    1907 **Tatters, a Tale of the Slums**
    1927 **Underworld,** directed by Josef von Sternberg, with George Bancroft (Paramount)

24. THE END OF THE SILENT ERA
    1928 **Plane Crazy,** the first Mickey Mouse, by Walt Disney (Disney)
    1928 **The Last Command,** directed by Josef von Sternberg, with Emil Jannings (Paramount)

25. THE TALKIES ARRIVE

1927   Scenes from **The Jazz Singer,** with Al Jolson (Warner Bros.)

1927   **Movietone Newsreel,** with George Bernard Shaw (Twentieth Century-Fox)

1930   **All Quiet on the Western Front,** directed by Lewis Milestone, with Louis Wolheim (Universal)

1928   **Steamboat Willie,** by Walt Disney (Walt Disney)

26. THE MUSICAL COMEDY FILM

1929   **The Love Parade,** directed by Ernst Lubitsch, with Maurice Chevalier and Jeanette MacDonald (Paramount)

27. THE GANGSTER FILM (II)

1930   **Little Caesar,** directed by Mervyn LeRoy, with Edward G. Robinson (Warner Bros.)

28. STAGE INTO SCREEN (II)

1930   **Anna Christie,** directed by Clarence Brown, with Greta Garbo and Marie Dressler (Loew's)

29. THE FILM AND CONTEMPORARY HISTORY

1935   **The March of Time, No. 2** (March of Time)

1933   **Cavalcade,** directed by Frank Lloyd, with Clive Brook and Diana Wynyard (Twentieth Century-Fox)

30. THE SOCIOLOGICAL FILM (II)

1932   **I Am a Fugitive from a Chain Gang,** directed by Mervyn LeRoy, with Paul Muni (Warner Bros.)

The names in parentheses are those of individuals and companies through whose courtesy and coöperation the Film Library has secured the films.

1915: D. W. Griffith's **The Birth of a Nation.**

1912: D. W. Griffith's **The New York Hat,** with Mary Pickford and Lionel Barry-more.

1914: Thomas H. Ince's **The Fugitive,** with William S. Hart.

1919: D. W. Griffith's **Broken Blossoms,** with Lillian Gish and Donald Crisp.

1919: Robert Wiene's **The Cabinet of Dr. Caligari.**

1922: Allan Dwan's **Robin Hood,** with Douglas Fairbanks.

1926: Robert Flaherty's **Moana of the South Seas.**

1924: Buster Keaton in **The Navigator.**

1925: Harold Lloyd in **The Freshman.**

1923: James Cruze's **The Covered Wagon.**

1923-4: Greta Garbo in Mauritz Stiller's
The Story of Gösta Berling.

1924: Emil Jannings in F. W. Murnau's **The Last Laugh.**

1925: King Vidor's **The Big Parade.**

1924: This animated figure of Chaplin occurs in **Ballet Mécanique,** the abstract film by the painter, Fernand Léger.

1929: From Walt Disney's first Silly Symphony. **The Skeleton Dance.**

356

1923: René Clair's first film, **The Crazy Ray.**

1923: Germaine Dulac's **The Smiling Madame Beudet.**

1927: Al Jolson in **The Jazz Singer.**

1929: Ernst Lubitsch's **The Love Parade,** with Jeanette MacDonald and Maurice Chevalier.

1927: F. W. Murnau's **Sunrise,** with Janet Gaynor and George O'Brien.

1930: Mervyn LeRoy's gangster film, **Little Caesar,** with Edward G. Robinson.

1932: Paul Muni in Mervyn LeRoy's **I Am a Fugitive from a Chain Gang.**

La grande Ourse.

GEORGES MÉLIÈS, MAGICIAN AND FILM PIONEER: 1861-1938

Films are made by men, not by machines or corporations, and in any history of the film's growth the personal and biographical element must bulk large. The work of the late Georges Méliès, for example, vividly illustrates a whole era of endeavor in the earliest years of the cinema. Others before him had discovered how to make moving pictures, but Méliès permanently enriched the technique and scope of the new medium by introducing it to fancy and to fantasy and by forcing it to tell a story. His films were true primitives of a new art.

The son of a well-to-do manufacturer in Paris, Méliès began his professional career in 1888 as proprietor and prin-cipal performer of the little Théâtre Robert-Houdin at 8, Boulevard des Italiens. It was one of those temples of conjuring and mystification, so popular in the last century, where automatons played whist and lady-assistants were sawn in half. Destiny contrived that he should be invited, late in the winter of 1895, to attend the historical first exhibition of films given by Auguste and Louis Lumière in the basement of a café near his theatre. All the audience marvelled but Méliès was spellbound: for him those 50-foot films of *Lunch-Hour at the Factory* and *Arrival of a Train*[1] were more than a semi-scientific novelty—they were a new kind of magic. He determined im-

[1] Both shown in program 12 of the Cycle of Seventy Films.

mediately to make films himself. Since the Lumières would not sell or rent him their *cinématographe*—in fact they warned him that he would ruin himself if he persisted in his intentions—he obtained a machine from R. W. Paul in London and by April 1896 had made his first picture and shown it at his theatre.

The Lumières were right: Méliès did eventually ruin himself. But before that happened he had produced hundreds of films and had oriented the motion picture in a new direction. At the outset his work resembled Lumière's—glimpses of the Méliès family at home, of street scenes in Paris. Then one day this practising magician accidentally discovered stop-motion cinematography. He realized how he could use it to create visual illusions on the screen and began making trick films. By the end of 1896 he was busily photographing *The Vanishing Lady*, *The Haunted Castle*, *A Nightmare* and similar subjects in the garden of his home at Montreuil. Wind and rain and changing sunlight soon drove him indoors. He designed a studio which looked like a conservatory but was in reality very like a theatre except that, instead of an audience, there was a camera to observe what took place on the "stage." *The Conjurer** is typical of his early studio work. Ambitious to create more splendid and complex effects, Méliès in 1900 finally hit upon the type of film which is peculiarly his with *Cinderella*—the first of a long line of fairy-tale subjects in which magical transformations occur in a succession of stage spectacles or tableaux linked by a narrative plot. He flung himself with childlike zest into the work of writing scenarios,

designing and painting scenery, drilling his little corps of helpers and artistes and appearing himself in the rich succession of "transformations, tricks, fairy-tales, apotheoses, artistic and fantastic scenes, comic subjects, war pictures, fantasies and illusions" which his letter-head of that time promised. They could all be obtained either plain or colored.

If it is as a master of trick-films and fantastic spectacles that Méliès is best remembered, by no means all his pictures were of that type. An awareness of political and topical events led him in 1899 to make a stark little *Dreyfus Affair* and an imaginative *Wreck of the Maine*. He re-created *The Coronation of King Edward VII* in his studio in 1902 for an English company and followed it in 1907 with *Long Distance Wireless Photography*. Unfortunately none of these has so far been recovered. *A Trip to the Moon**, his most famous picture, was made in 1902, a year earlier than Edwin S. Porter's even more famous (and fundamentally more cinematic) *Great Train Robbery*. By the time his last "big" film, *The Conquest of the Pole**, appeared in 1912 other men had developed the motion picture in ways unknown to Méliès. A really flexible form of narrative film was shaping in America, so that between D. W. Griffith's *New York Hat* (1912) and the work of Méliès there is already an infinite distance. But it was Méliès who had paved the way. Though he certainly regarded the film as a branch of theatre art, though his style is monotonous and his screen cramped, his films themselves are instinct with two vital elements—movement and imagination. The crude but effective dis-

* An asterisk following the title of a film indicates that it will be shown in a fifty-minute program of Méliès' films to be given in the Museum auditorium throughout the summer. See page 366.

362

solves which link together the successive tableaux of *A Trip to the Moon* and the astonishing close-up of the moon's face gliding toward the camera were both of them distinct creations. If today we most appreciate the period flavor and quaintness of his work it need not be with any forgetfulness of his contributions or of the world-wide success his films once enjoyed. Actually, in his predilection for the fantastic and the dream-like, he seems to anticipate the irrational imagery of the Surrealists.

The end of Méliès' story is sad. His method of operation was costly and the fact that he sold prints of his films instead of renting them left the profits in the hands of others. He was a victim of the illegal duping of films so prevalent in the early years of the cinema and the New York office which he set up in an effort to prevent just such thefts turned out in the end to be a liability instead of an asset. In 1914 the war put a stop to his career as a producer: in 1925 he lost both the Montreuil property and the Théâtre Robert-Houdin, destroyed all the films in his possession and vanished into obscurity. Some belated glory came his way after 1929 when he was found selling toys and candy in a little stand at the Gare Montparnasse: he was feted and publicized. Though his circumstances remained straitened, in 1931 he was made a Chevalier of the Légion d'Honneur and, in the same year, was also granted admission to the French film industry's Maison de Retraite at Orly, eight miles outside Paris. Here in a corner of a large empty mansion set in ornamental grounds he spent the last years of his life, executing from memory many replicas of the scenery in his old films, receiving gladly such visitors as called to pay their respects to a pioneer of the world's most popular and lucrative art and hoped to be actively employed again. He died, still hoping, on January 22nd, 1938.

Though most of Méliès' films have vanished there is still a chance that others than those now visible may yet turn up. Meanwhile the great wealth of sketches, drawings, still photographs and other documents which have been preserved makes it possible to study his method and almost to visualize the missing films. In them we catch a glimpse of a versatile and ingenious spirit wrestling with a new medium. They breathe forth the unmistakable atmosphere of 19th century Paris, of its popular theatres patronized by a petty bourgeoisie familiar with Jules Verne and Offenbach and Doré, fascinated alike by white magic and by semi-scientific curiosities and well able, therefore, to accept the skilful distillation from these sources which Méliès combined in his "vues fantastiques."

Grateful acknowledgment is made to Madame Georges Méliès for the loan of the greater part of the material included in the gallery exposition, as well as to MM. Henry Langlois and Georges Franju of the Cinémathèque Française and to Miss Olwen Vaughan of the British Film Institute through whose mediation the loan of the documents was secured.

I. B.

363

The Merry Frolics of Satan, 1906.

A magic steed and vehicle from one of Méliès' many trick films.

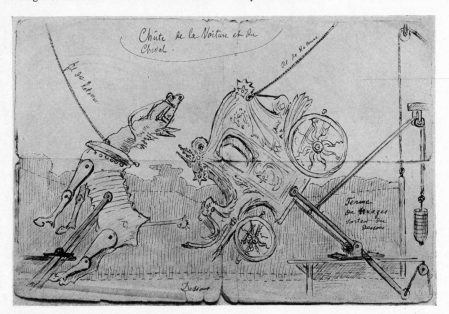

The Merry Frolics of Satan, 1906.

Méliès' sketch for the above.

The Land of Toys, 1908.

One of Méliès' dainty tableaux, modeled on stage spectacles of the 19th century.

The Conquest of the Pole, 1912.

A scene from Méliès' last "big" film, showing one of his ingeniously painted backgrounds.

Five Fantastic Films by Georges Méliès to be shown in the Museum auditorium throughout the summer

1899 **The Conjurer,** with Méliès as the Conjurer (acquired through the courtesy of the British Film Institute)

1902 **A Trip to the Moon** (Le Voyage dans la Lune), with Méliès as the Inventor, dancers from the Théâtre du Châtelet, acrobats from the Folies Bergères (from the Will Day and Jean A. LeRoy Collections)

1905 **The Palace of the Arabian Nights** (Le Palais des Mille et Une Nuits) (from the Jean A. LeRoy Collection)

1908 **The Doctor's Secret** (Hydrothérapie Fantastique), with Méliès as the Doctor (from the Jean A. LeRoy Collection)

1912 **Conquest of the Pole** (A la Conquête du Pôle), with Méliès as Engineer Maboul (acquired through the courtesy of the British Film Institute)

All the above films were conceived, written, designed and directed by Georges Méliès, and produced by his company, Star-Film, Paris.

366

DESIGNS FOR AN ABSTRACT FILM: A Pre-War Experiment

The two sets of abstract designs in gouache now on exhibition were evolved as the basis for a film project, together with two or more additional sets, in and after 1913 by the Cubist painter, Léopold Survage.[1] The paintings themselves are of the same nature as the master-drawings for an animated cartoon which, when the whole design is finally to be executed, are copied on celluloid sheets by assistant-draftsmen who also supply the missing transitions between the key drawings so as to create a smooth and continuous movement on the screen. The use of this method was assumed by Survage, as was also the use of a three-color camera to photograph the designs.[2]

Survage gave to his work in this field the name of *Le Rhythme Coloré*, regarding it as a new variety of artistic expression analogous to musical composition but employing a succession of colored forms instead of a succession of sounds. He was led to experiment in this fashion out of disappointment with the limitations which, he felt at that time, were imposed on abstract painting; but it is probable that he was considerably influenced, also, by the interest and enthusiasm for motion pictures in general displayed by associates in Paris like Maurice Raynal and Guillaume Apollinaire. When the present paintings and others were exhibited in 1917, Apollinaire wrote the foreword to the catalog, recounting how Survage had labored at the work of preparation for years while earning a meagre livelihood as a piano-tuner and how, finally, the promised execution of the project had been stopped by the outbreak of war.

The artist furnished both indications of his theory and a description of his intent in the article in *Les Soirées de Paris* already referred to. "An immobile abstract form does not say much," is his rather challenging statement, ". . . it is only when it sets in motion, when it is transformed and meets other forms, that it becomes capable of evoking a feeling . . . Upon becoming transformed in time, it sweeps space; it encounters other forms in the path of its transformation and they combine; sometimes they travel side by side, and sometimes battle among themselves or dance to the cadenced rhythm that directs them . . . the transformations begin anew, and it is in this way that visual rhythm becomes analogous to the sound-rhythm of music."[3]

[1] Survage, né Sturzwage. Born Moscow, 1879. Lives in Paris.
[2] *Les Soirées de Paris*, 26/7, July-Aug. 1914, pp. 426-429.
[3] Tr. by Samuel Putnam. *Transition* 6, Sept. 1927, pp. 180-184.

SURVAGE: Sequence of six paintings in gouache, part of a project for *Colored Rhythm,* an abstract film. 1913

In the history of motion pictures, Survage's *Colored Rhythms* constitute a pioneer effort. He was the first to attempt an abstract film and to translate into practice (almost before they were formed) the theories of the French advance-guard critics and the Italian Futurists on the properties and functions of the film as a medium for esthetic expression. It was not until 1919 that the first abstract films were actually produced: *Diagonal-Symphonie* by Viking Eggeling (1879-1925), a Swedish painter with French affinities resident in Berlin; *Prelude* by his co-worker, Hans Richter, and *Opus I, II and III* by another German painter, now an eminent film director, Walter Ruttmann. The best known of all abstract films, however, is undoubtedly Fernand Léger's *Ballet Mécanique* (1924).

Most nearly akin to Survage's project, however, are the abstract color-films of the Australian painter, Len Lye, whose *Colour Box* (1935), *Rainbow Dance* (1936) and *Trade Tattoo* (1937) were issued as advertisements by the General Post Office of Great Britain. Another worker in this medium, Oskar Fischinger, who produced a number of abstract films in Germany both in black and white and in color between 1928 and 1932, subsequently made *Optical Poem* for Metro-Goldwyn-Mayer and has recently joined the staff of artists at the Walt Disney studio in Hollywood.

I. B.

INDEX

Except where reference to a page is given, figures refer to catalog numbers.

370

ADVERTISEMENTS

FILMS
PUBLICATIONS
COLOR REPRODUCTIONS
CIRCULATING EXHIBITIONS

THE MUSEUM OF MODERN ART
11 WEST 53RD ST. NEW YORK

FILMS

The Museum of Modern Art Film Library exists for the purpose of collecting and preserving representative moving pictures of all kinds, as well as related material, with the purpose of making them available for study. In order to make possible examination of the films themselves, a circulating library of film programs has been created which is at the disposal of colleges, museums and study groups. Six series of film programs are now prepared which provide a provisional review of the history, the technical and esthetic development of the moving picture in the United States and in three foreign countries. Most of these programs are included in the "Cycle of Seventy Films" (see pages 345-348). Forthcoming series will review the film in other countries and supplement the present material. Program notes accompany each film, and the Film Library also provides a simple piano score to accompany each program.

The Film Library is the custodian and not the owner of the films in these circulating programs. There are, in consequence, certain conditions which must be met before any program can be sent out to an institution or study group wishing to exhibit it. The conditions can be learned from the Film Library.

PUBLICATIONS

The publications of the Museum of Modern Art are for the most part issued in connection with its exhibitions. They are also intended to be useful in themselves. For this reason they are profusely illustrated and include a good deal of explanatory text. Concerned with the entire range of modern art and many of its sources in the art of the past, they deal not only with painting and sculpture but also with architecture, industrial art, theatre art, photography and films.

Because the Museum is a non-profit-making institution it has been possible to sell these books at a price far lower than that which would be set by a commercial publisher. In addition, certain discounts are offered. Members of the Museum, who receive four books a year as part of their membership privilege, are permitted to purchase other Museum publications at a discount of 25%. A discount of 20% is allowed libraries, museums, educational institutions and teachers and students. Sixteen out-of-print titles are not included in the following list.

Recently the Museum has also begun to publish color reproductions. Two portfolios, the contents of which are listed below, are being issued in connection with this Tenth Anniversary Exhibition. Several other color reproductions are also available. Museums, libraries, educational institutions and teachers and students receive a 25% discount on the color reproductions.

PAINTING AND SCULPTURE, GENERAL

Fantastic Art, Dada, Surrealism

Edited by Alfred H. Barr, Jr., with two essays by Georges Hugnet

Fantastic subject matter has persisted in European art from the middle ages to the present day. The text and 222 illustrations trace this tradition from the 15th century through Dada and Surrealism, the two principal movements concerned in our own time with the marvelous and the anti-rational.

296 pages; 222 plates; $3.00

Masters of Popular Painting (Modern Primitives of Europe and America)

Text by Holger Cahill, Maximilien Gauthier, Jean Cassou, Dorothy C. Miller and others

Masters of Popular Painting presents the work of twenty-two "self-taught" "artists of the people." Full biographies of all the artists add warmth and color to the critical essays, and the illustrations, including two color plates, present a delightful picture-book survey of a major division of modern art.

172 pages; 80 plates; 2 color plates; $2.50

Modern Painters and Sculptors as Illustrators

By Monroe Wheeler

A study of books illustrated by major 20th century artists and a few of their 19th century predecessors.

116 pages; 70 plates; $1.50

Modern Works of Art

Edited and with an introduction by Alfred H. Barr, Jr.

A pictorial anthology of modern painting, and sculpture, including brief biographies of 111 artists.

152 pages; 147 plates; $2.50

The Lillie P. Bliss Collection

Edited by Alfred H. Barr, Jr., with an essay on Cézanne by Jerome Klein

The *catalogue raisonné* of one of the most important private collections of modern painting in the world, bequeathed to the Museum several years ago.

164 pages; 93 plates; paper bound; $1.50

PRIMITIVE AND EXOTIC ARTS

Prehistoric Rock Pictures in Europe and Africa

By Professor Leo Frobenius and Douglas C. Fox.

Painted and engraved by people who lived from 500 to 20,000 years ago, these rock pictures bring to life two separate prehistoric cultures.

82 pages; 38 illustrations; $1.85

Aztec, Incan and Mayan Art

By Holger Cahill

The art of the ancient civilizations of America. Formerly titled: **American Sources of Modern Art.**

104 pages; 56 plates; paper bound $1.50

African Negro Art

By James Johnson Sweeney

An account of one of the major esthetic discoveries of the 20th century. One hundred plates reproduce sculptured figures and ceremonial masks of wood, bronze and ivory.

144 pages; 100 plates; $2.50

PAINTING AND SCULPTURE, EUROPEAN

Cézanne, Gauguin, Seurat, van Gogh

The four painters of the 19th century who have been chiefly honored by the painters of the 20th as pioneers of modern art, men who founded new traditions and rediscovered old ones. With an essay by Alfred H. Barr, Jr.

152 pages; 97 plates; paper bound, $2.00

Painting in Paris

A succinct introduction to the work of the School of Paris, the most influential group of living artists, headed by Bonnard, Braque, Derain, Matisse, Picasso, Miro, de Chirico. With notes by Alfred H. Barr, Jr.

88 pages; 50 plates; paper bound $1.50

German Painting and Sculpture

By Alfred H. Barr, Jr.
The development of modern German art from Expressionism to the New Objectivity. Included is the work of the leading German painters and sculptors, almost all of whom are now officially out of favor in their own country.

91 pages; 49 plates; paper bound $1.50

Vincent van Gogh

Edited by Alfred H. Barr, Jr.
An artist's life set down as he revealed it in letters to his intimates. A frontispiece in full color, sixty full page reproductions of van Gogh's oils and twenty reproductions of watercolors and drawings.

193 pages; 84 plates; $2.50

Letters of Vincent van Gogh to Emile Bernard

Translated and edited by Douglas Lord
Letters to a fellow artist, probably the most memorable which van Gogh wrote. Sketches of paintings in the letters are reproduced in facsimile facing reproductions of the finished pictures. With an introduction and scholarly notes.

124 pages; 32 plates; $2.50

PAINTING AND SCULPTURE, AMERICAN

New Horizons in American Art

Edited by Dorothy C. Miller, with an essay by Holger Cahill
A report to the public of one year's activity of the Federal Art Project, showing murals, easel paintings, posters, prints and children's work, and providing "an illuminating history of American art in relation to society."

176 pages; 102 plates; $2.50

Paintings by Nineteen Living Americans

The painters represented are: Burchfield, Demuth, Dickinson, Feininger, Hart, Hopper, Karfiol, Kent, Kuhn, Kuniyoshi, Lawson, Marin, Miller, O'Keeffe, Pascin, Sloan, Speicher, Sterne, Weber.

88 pages; 38 plates; paper bound $1.50

Painting and Sculpture from 16 American Cities

With biographical notes by Alfred H. Barr, Jr.
61 pages; 116 plates; paper bound $1.00

American Folk Art, 1750-1900: The Art of the Common Man in America

By Holger Cahill

The most comprehensive survey yet published of the American folk-art tradition, with emphasis on painting and sculpture rather than on the crafts.

131 pages; 80 plates; paper bound $1.50

Trois Siècles d'Art aux Etats-Unis

With essays by Alfred H. Barr, Jr., John McAndrew, Beaumont Newhall and Iris Barry, and a foreword by A. Conger Goodyear.

An exhibition of painting, sculpture, graphic arts, architecture, photography and films, organized by the Museum of Modern Art at the invitation of the French Government and shown at the Musée du Jeu de Paume, Paris.

210 pages; 103 plates; paper bound

John Marin

With essays by Henry McBride, Marsden Hartley and E. M. Benson

Six full color plates and forty-one halftone reproductions are supplemented by three critical essays which supply a rich and varied estimate of a great contemporary American.

102 pages; 47 plates; $2.50

Charles Burchfield, Early Watercolors

Edited and with an introduction by Alfred H. Barr, Jr., notes by Charles Burchfield

The fantastic early work of the distinguished painter of American streets and houses.

24 pages; 10 plates; paper bound $1.00

Max Weber

With notes by Max Weber and an introduction by Alfred H. Barr, Jr.

A pioneer of American modernism.

40 pages; 16 plates; paper bound $1.00

Edward Hopper

With essays by Edward Hopper and Charles Burchfield and an introduction by Alfred H. Barr, Jr.

81 pages; 48 plates; paper bound $1.00

George Caleb Bingham

With essays by Meyric C. Rogers, James B. Musick and Arthur Pope.

"The Missouri Artist," whose paintings of Mississippi River life and political campaigns anticipated the current interest in the American scene.

32 pages; 14 plates; paper bound $3.00

Gaston Lachaise

With an essay by Lincoln Kirstein.

The life and work of one of the most important sculptors of our period.

64 pages; 44 plates; paper bound $1.00

ARCHITECTURE AND INDUSTRIAL ART

Bauhaus 1919-1933

Edited by Herbert Bayer, Walter Gropius, Ise Gropius

A survey of the work of the most important twentieth century school of design. Through its director, its teachers and its students, the Bauhaus has exerted a far-reaching influence on contemporary architecture and industrial art.

224 pages; 550 plates; $3.75

376

Modern Architecture

With essays by Lewis Mumford, Henry-Russell Hitchcock, Jr. and Philip Johnson, and a foreword by Alfred H. Barr, Jr.

The development and extent of modern architecture with biographies and chronologies of a dozen leading architects.

200 pages; 65 plates; paper bound $1.50

Modern Architecture in England

With essays by Henry-Russell Hitchcock, Jr. and Catherine K. Bauer

Some of the most exciting developments in modern architecture today are taking place in England. Fifty photographs and plans of outstanding new buildings supplement the historical and critical material of the two essays.

104 pages; 53 plates; $1.85

The New Architecture and the Bauhaus

By Walter Gropius, with an introduction by Joseph Hudnut

Professor Gropius, founder of the Bauhaus and now a Professor at Harvard University, analyzes here the nature of the Bauhaus contribution.

90 pages; 16 plates; $1.75

The Architecture of H. H. Richardson and His Times

By Henry-Russell Hitchcock, Jr.

An historical and critical analysis of the work of the great 19th century American, the last major architect to work with traditional materials and one of the first to be preoccupied with the functional problems of modern building.

511 pages; 145 plates; $6.00

Louis Sullivan, Prophet of Modern Architecture

By Hugh Morrison

Louis Sullivan's technical and esthetic achievements, especially as a pioneer in skyscraper design, make him a figure important to every student of American culture.

Published in collaboration with W. W. Norton and Co.

330 pages; 100 illustrations; $4.00

Machine Art

Edited by Philip Johnson with a foreword by Alfred H. Barr, Jr.

A brief article on the history and principles of design in machine-manufactured products precedes the illustrated sections in which are pictured machine parts, household and office equipment, kitchenware and household furnishings, etc.

116 pages; 121 plates; paper bound $1.50

Alvar Aalto—Architecture and Furniture

With essays by Simon Breines and A. Lawrence Kocher

The first American survey of the work of Alvar Aalto, one of the most original and successful architects of the present decade, the designer of the brilliant Finnish pavilion at the New York World's Fair.

52 pages; 35 halftones and plans; bound in boards $1.00

Posters by Cassandre

Foreword by Ernestine M. Fantl

A monograph on the distinguished French commercial artist.

16 pages; 9 plates; paper bound $.25

Posters by E. McKnight Kauffer

Foreword by Aldous Huxley

Aldous Huxley identifies those qualities which have made E. McKnight Kauffer one of the leading poster designers of our time.

28 pages; 12 plates; paper bound, $.50

Ignatz Wiemeler, Modern Bookbinder

Foreword by Monroe Wheeler, with an essay by Professor Wiemeler

16 pages; 9 plates; paper bound $.50

PHOTOGRAPHY AND FILMS

Photography, A Short Critical History

By Beaumont Newhall

The only history available in English which describes the rise of photography as both a science and an art. Included are discussions of news, color and scientific photography and the moving picture.

225 pages; 95 plates; $3.00

American Photographs

By Walker Evans with an essay by Lincoln Kirstein

Reproductions of the work of one of the foremost American photographers.

198 pages; 87 plates; $2.50

The History of Motion Pictures

By Maurice Bardèche and Robert Brasillach; translated and edited by Iris Barry

An international survey of the cinema, tracing its history in Europe and America and analyzing the influence on films of great directors and famous stars.

Published in collaboration with W. W. Norton and Co.

412 pages; 30 plates; $4.00

COLOR REPRODUCTIONS OF MODERN PAINTINGS

Art in Our Time Portfolios: The extraordinarily low price of the two portfolios listed below has been made possible by large editions and the generous assistance of Fortune Magazine and the Condé Nast Publications which have permitted the Museum to reprint from some of their color plates. The average size of the prints is 8 x 10 inches on formats 11¼ x 14 inches.

Portfolio Number One

at Museum desk **$1.00**

1. **Pierre BONNARD: The Breakfast Room.** Stephen C. Clark Collection, New York
2. **Paul CEZANNE: Man in a Blue Cap** (Uncle Dominic). About 1865. The Museum of Modern Art, the Lillie P. Bliss Collection
3. **Paul GAUGUIN: The Spirit of the Dead Watching** (Manaò Tupapaù). 1892. A. Conger Goodyear Collection, New York
4. **Vincent van GOGH: L'Arlésienne** (Mme. Ginoux). 1888. The Lewisohn Collection, New York
5. **Winslow HOMER: The Croquet Match.** 1872. Edwin S. Webster Collection, Boston

378

6. **Henri-MATISSE: White Plumes.** 1919. Stephen C. Clark Collection, New York
7. **Pablo PICASSO: Youth Leading a Horse.** 1905. William S. Paley Collection, New York
8. **Auguste RENOIR: Le Moulin de la Galette.** 1876. John Hay Whitney Collection, New York

Portfolio Number Two   at Museum desk **$1.00**

1. **Hans ARP: Mountain, Table, Anchors, Navel.** 1925. The Museum of Modern Art, given anonymously
2. **Peter BLUME: Parade.** 1930. The Museum of Modern Art, Mrs. John D. Rockefeller, Jr. Collection
3. **Camille BOMBOIS: Before Entering the Ring.** Mme. E. Hostettler Collection, Berne
4. **Georges BRAQUE: Still Life.** 1928. Frank Crowninshield Collection, New York
5. **Charles BURCHFIELD: The Night Wind.** 1918. A. Conger Goodyear Collection, New York
6. **Giorgio de CHIRICO: Nostalgia of the Infinite.** 1911. The Museum of Modern Art, given anonymously
7. **Salvador DALI: Portrait of Gala.** 1935. The Museum of Modern Art, given anonymously
8. **Juan GRIS: The Chessboard.** 1917. The Museum of Modern Art, Mrs. John D. Rockefeller, Jr. Purchase Fund
9. **Edward HOPPER: House by the Railroad.** 1925. The Museum of Modern Art, gift of Stephen C. Clark
10. **John KANE: Self Portrait.** 1929. The Museum of Modern Art, Mrs. John D. Rockefeller, Jr. Purchase Fund
11. **Paul KLEE: A Gay Repast.** 1928. Private Collection, New York
12. **Piet MONDRIAN: Composition in Black, White and Red.** 1936. The Museum of Modern Art, gift of the Advisory Committee
13. **José Clemente OROZCO: Zapatistas.** 1931. The Museum of Modern Art, given anonymously
14. **Pablo PICASSO: The Mirror.** 1932. The Museum of Modern Art, gift of Mrs. Simon Guggenheim
15. **Grant WOOD: Daughters of Revolution.** 1932. Edward G. Robinson Collection, Beverly Hills.

Diego RIVERA:

While the Poor Sleep (Fresco in Ministry of Education, Mexico City), 11 x 9 inches   **$3.00**

Cane Workers (Fresco in Palace of Cortez, Cuernavaca), 11 x 9 inches   **3.00**

Emiliano Zapata (Fresco in Palace of Cortez, Cuernavaca), 11 x 9 inches   **3.00**

Joseph PICKETT: Manchester Valley, 8 x 6 inches   **$.25**

Henri ROUSSEAU: Basket of Flowers, 7 x 5¾ inches   **.25**

Color Postcards of Paintings in the Museum's Collection

1. **Paul CEZANNE: Man in a Blue Cap.** About 1865   .10
2. **Salvador DALI: The Persistence of Memory.** 1931   .10
3. **Charles DEMUTH: Acrobats.** 1919   .10
4. **John MARIN: Camden Mountain Across the Bay.** 1922   .10
5. **Henri-MATISSE: Bather.** About 1908   .10
6. **Pablo PICASSO: Green Still Life.** 1914   .10
7. **Maurice PRENDERGAST: April Snow, Salem.** 1906-07   .10
8. **Georges SEURAT: Two Dancers.** About 1882   .10

Reproductions of a Larger Size

Pablo PICASSO: Woman in White. 1923. The Museum of Modern Art, the Lillie P. Bliss Collection   **$1.00**

An "offset" color reproduction 15 x 18½ inches on format 20 x 26 inches published in an edition of sufficient size to make the price of $1.00 possible

Paul CEZANNE: The Card Players. 1892. Stephen C. Clark Collection   **$3.00**

A colotype print 13½ x 17 inches on format 17½ x 22 inches

Auguste RENOIR: Little Margot Bérard. 1879. Stephen C. Clark Collection   **$3.00**

A colotype print 12½ x 16 inches on format 17½ x 22 inches

(The two colotypes, Renoir's *Little Margot Bérard* and Cézanne's *The Card Players*, are sold at $2.00 each within the Museum and at $1.00 to members of the Museum)

CIRCULATING EXHIBITIONS

The Museum has been sending its exhibitions on tour throughout the country since 1931. From two traveling exhibitions, the department has expanded this educational service to more than thirty exhibitions offered annually to museums, colleges, schools and clubs which can meet the requirements concerning display, care in packing and handling, adequate protection against fire and theft.

Many museums in other leading cities show the Museum's major exhibitions after the New York showing. In addition to the exhibitions held at the Museum, collections are assembled for tour which are especially adapted for colleges and schools or organizations interested in promoting an understanding and appreciation of modern art. Careful biographical and explanatory notes accompany these collections. Museum catalogs are offered at discounts to exhibitors. Publicity information and photographs are supplied. The collections are packed ready for installation so that a minimum of work is necessary to set up each exhibition. Complete packing, unpacking and installation instructions are sent with each show. Rental fees include all expenses except one-way transportation charges from the last point on the itinerary.

Currently the following exhibitions are available. Announcement of approximately fifteen new shows will be made in the catalog to be published by the Department of Circulating Exhibitions by May 15, 1939. Certain of the exhibitions on this list will be removed from circulation.

PAINTINGS, DRAWINGS AND PRINTS — Rental Fee

Masters of Popular Painting
$500 4 weeks

Modern Primitives of Europe and America—75 paintings

Three Mexican Artists
50 2 weeks

Six important paintings by Mexico's leading modern artists: Rivera, Orozco, Siqueiros

War in Spain
60 3 weeks

One hundred pen and ink drawings by Luis Quintanilla

Prehistoric Rock Pictures
200 3 weeks

125 facsimiles of man's earliest paintings from the Frobenius Collection

Comparative Styles in Europe and Africa of Prehistoric Rock Pictures
35 3 weeks

A collection of 39 facsimiles assembled especially for schools and colleges

Paintings and Sculpture by Children
30 3 weeks

A selection of work by children from 4 to 16 taken from the Museum's Permanent Collection and the Federal Art Project

War Etchings by Goya and Dix
30 2 weeks

50 prints from Goya's "Desastros de la Guerra" and 50 prints from Dix' portfolio "Der Krieg"

The Prints of Georges Rouault
75 3 weeks

85 large etchings, lithographs and woodcuts, some in color, many of them never before exhibited

The American Scene
30 2 weeks

Etchings, lithographs and woodcuts from the collection of Mrs. John D. Rockefeller, Jr.

381

Masters of the School of Paris $30 2 weeks

Etchings, drypoints, and lithographs, some in color from the collection
of Mrs. John D. Rockefeller, Jr.

Twenty-five Watercolors by American Artists   50 3 weeks

Selections from the Museum's Permanent Collection.

Twenty-five Drawings by European and American Artists   30 3 weeks

Selections from the Museum's Permanent Collection.

ARCHITECTURE

Bauhaus: 1919-1928   375 4 weeks

The work of masters and students from the most important school of
design of the twentieth century

The Bauhaus: How It Worked   75 3 weeks

A smaller collection of original and photographic material for colleges
and schools illustrating the Bauhaus system of education

Three Centuries of American Architecture   175 3 weeks

Photographs, charts, models and a film illustrate the development of
native and imported building traditions from 1609 to 1938

Alvar Aalto: Architecture and Furniture   75 3 weeks

A retrospective exhibition including photographs, drawings, models,
furniture and glassware by one of the most important and original
modern architects and furniture designers of the past decade

What is Modern Architecture?   12 2 weeks

Photographs, charts, diagrams and text discussing planning, construction, materials and the problems of designing a modern building

Modern American Houses   25 2 weeks

An explanation of the modern house with photographs, plans and text
from architects and owners on "how it works"

A New House by Frank Lloyd Wright   15 2 weeks

Photographs and plans of a recently completed house at Bear Run,
Pennsylvania, affirm Wright's place among the world leaders in modern
architecture

Modern Architecture in England   75 3 weeks

In the last five years England has become one of the leaders in modern
architecture. The exhibition represents work of its foremost architects

382

Henry Hobson Richardson (1836-1886) $30 3 weeks

One of America's greatest architects, Richardson forecast many of the principles of modern architecture. The exhibition shows the development of his style by means of plans, photographs and drawings

Le Corbusier   30 3 weeks

Enlarged photographs, plans and one model illustrate Le Corbusier's theories of planning and designing

Competition Drawings for a Fine Arts Center at Wheaton College, Norton, Mass.   15 2 weeks

Competition Drawings for a Festival Theatre and Fine Arts Department at William and Mary College, Virginia.   15 2 weeks

Houses and Housing   fee to be announced

The contributions of modern architecture to modern living

Housing   fee to be announced

A survey of the development of housing in Europe and America. An inexpensive exhibition for schools and colleges.

The Evolution of the Skyscraper   10 single showing
25 2 weeks with exhibition

A 45 minute movie on 16 mm. film. Supplemented by an exhibition of approximately 20 photographs

INDUSTRIAL ART

Posters by E. McKnight Kauffer   25 2 weeks

50 examples of advertising art by England's foremost designer

Government Posters   12 2 weeks

A comparison of Government sponsored poster design in Spain and the United States

Machine Art   50 4 weeks

Machine parts and products selected for beauty of form and design

Useful Objects under $5.00   50 3 weeks

Modern household furnishings and accessories designed for industrial production

PHOTOGRAPHY

American Photographs by Walker Evans $50 4 weeks

The first one-man photography exhibition given by the Museum. Includes 100 prints

Documents of America: The Rural Scene 25 3 weeks

A selection of work from the Farm Security Administration

COLOR PRODUCTIONS

An Introduction to Modern Painting 30 3 weeks

40 pictures showing revolutionary changes in art history from 1830 to 1900

Twentieth Century Painting In Europe 30 3 weeks

The important movements including Fauvism, Expressionism, Futurism, Cubism, Abstract Art, Surrealism, New Realism and mural painting since 1900

Paul Cézanne 30 2 weeks

A history of his work with biographical notes by Jerome Klein. 30 pictures including facsimiles of watercolors and oils

van Gogh 25 2 weeks

A comprehensive survey including 25 reproductions of oils, 5 of drawings and watercolors with biographical information, critical notes and quotations from the artist's letters

Modern Watercolors and Pastels 25 3 weeks

26 pictures illustrating the characteristic styles of leading European and American artists

American Painting 15 2 weeks

From the seventeenth century to the present day. 12 pictures with notes on each artist by leading art critics

FILMS

A Survey of the American Film 25 2 weeks

Two hundred stills from 1895 to 1938 illustrating changes and development in the American motion picture

The Making of a Contemporary Film—"The Adventures of Tom Sawyer" 35 2 weeks

Photographs, charts, reports, script and scenario show the step by step process of making a modern motion picture

384